A. Poulin, Jr.

SELECTED POEMS

A. POULIN, JR.

SELECTED POEMS

Edited, with an Introduction,
by Michael Waters

AMERICAN POETS CONTINUUM SERIES VOL. 66

BOA Editions, Ltd. ◼ Rochester, NY ◼ 2001

00 01 02 03 7 6 5 4 3 2 1

Publications by BOA Editions, Ltd. — a not-for-profit corporation un-
der section 501 (c) (3) of the United States Internal Revenue Code —
are made possible with the assistance of grants from the Literature
Program of the New York State Council on the Arts, the Literature
Program of the National Endowment for the Arts, the Sonia Raiziss
Giop Charitable Foundation, The Chase Manhattan Foundation,
as well as from the Mary S. Mulligan Charitable Trust, the
County of Monroe, NY, and The CIRE Foundation.

See page 208 for special individual acknowledgments.

LIBRARY OF CONGRESS CATALOGING-IN-PUBLICATION DATA
Poulin, A.
[Poems. Selections]
Selected poems / A. Poulin, Jr.; edited with an
introduction by Michael Waters.
p. cm. — (American poets continuum series; no 66)
ISBN 1-929918-02-x (alk. paper) — ISBN 1-929918-03-8 (pbk: alk. paper)
I. Waters, Michael, 1949– II. Title.
III. American poets continuum series; vol. 66
PS3566.O78 A6 2001
811'.54 — dc21   2001025597

BOA Editions, Ltd.
Steven Huff, Publisher
Richard Garth, Chair, Board of Directors
A. Poulin, Jr., President & Founder (1976–1996)
260 East Avenue
Rochester, NY 14604
www.boaeditions.org

NATIONAL
ENDOWMENT
FOR THE ARTS

State of the Arts

NYSCA

CONTENTS

PART III

Angelic Orders: A Bestiary of Angels

❂

PART IV

Letters from the Tower

✠

PART V

✠

vii

A. Poulin, Jr.

SELECTED POEMS

INTRODUCTION

" The purpose of poetry," wrote Milan Kundera, "is not to try to dazzle us with an astonishing thought, but to make one moment of existence unforgettable and worthy of unbearable nostalgia." Before his death, following chronic illness, on June 5, 1996, A. Poulin, Jr. crafted poems that managed many such moments.

Ambitious for the art rather than for himself, Poulin loved other poets' work as much as his own. He took sensual pleasure in the sound of words, in their texture as they spun in his mouth. He spoke of poetry as he spoke of food. His description of meals would make your mouth water and, at the same time, fill you with regret because there had never before *been* such meals, and never would be again. He'd speak with the same erotic fullness of a poem, so that you'd long to have that poem near you, lodged within you, a necessary sustenance. How could a body live without such food, without such poetry?

Yet Poulin also evinced an unself-conscious Puritan ethic in the work accomplished from his sickbed in his small upstate-New York village: by the *whump* you would have heard had you dropped his manuscripts onto your table. With books of his own rigorous poems, with widely praised translations of Rainer Maria Rilke and Anne Hébert, with everexpanding editions of his popular anthology, *Contemporary American Poetry*, and with prize-winning volumes published by the not-for-profit literary press he'd founded, BOA Editions, Ltd., Poulin assumed Walt Whitman's incumbent task: "Dazzling and tremendous how quick the sun-rise would kill me, / If I could not now and always send sun-rise out of me."

That rough-hewn Yankee pragmatism, originating in the manual labor of his forebears — farmers and fishermen — balanced his suburban epiphanies. As his poems deepened in intellectual and emotional complexity, in spiritual resonance, as his syllables approached rapturous

3

utterance, he developed a knotty syntax within strict stanzaic structures to ground his work. In a statement dated July 19, 1986, Poulin wrote:

> Although I've become increasingly intent on incorporating many of the more traditional qualities of poetry in my work — urgency, passion, intensity and richness of language, variations on formal and organic forms, music — I write from no predetermined or circumscribed aesthetic formula... I hope that each successful poem will be its own incarnate statement of poetics....

He went on:

> My subjects continue to shift from my French-Canadian, Roman-Catholic experience as a child and adolescent in a small rural town in Maine to my present diurnal experiences as (I hope) a mature lover, husband, father, artist and intellectual. (For the artist and intellectual, of course, ideas and states of being are as tangible and sensual as sex, lobster and gin.) But whether dealing with reverie or with more immediate existential reality, such as the threat of a nuclear holocaust, I work for ways to give my subjects viable images of themselves and a music that will redeem them, not only from the indifferent deterioration of objective entropy, but also from the more pernicious deterioration of language as symptomatic of our too common human and spiritual desolation.

Finally, he wrote of the importance of rooting his poems "in the substrata of the most fundamental reality that can be recognized by readers who know and feel what the quality and consequences of our remembered and daily lives are and can be. And poetry at that level heals and redeems, at once a deeply political and spiritual act."

Critics praised his accomplishment. Kathleen Norris wrote that his poems were "religious and political in the most profound sense," and that Poulin was "often unsettling in the way he [saw] ordinary life through the lens of eternity." *Library Journal* noted that Poulin had managed "some of the most profoundly religious poems written in modern times." Sensualist, moralist, "wingless, unfeathered," A. Poulin, Jr. was a poet consumed by our inability to reclaim grace and by our terrible desire for its consolations.

Michael Waters

SALISBURY, MARYLAND
JANUARY 2001

✠ ✠ ✠ ✠ ✠ ✠ ✠

PART I

The Front Parlor

Whenever someone in our family
died, the wake was in our house,
downstairs, in the front parlor.

It was a spare room, really, and,
except for a few extra folding chairs,
empty and unheated. The shades were

always drawn, the best lace curtains
hung. And in that constant cool
twilight, the wallpaper damp

as banks of carnations, when we
dared to go in, forbidden to,
we played like shadows under

the great cross, the enormous
suffering, dying or dead Christ,
the room's only constant ornament.

It never was a living room.

✠   ✠   ✠

I've slept above the dead before,
my bed in the same far corner
as their caskets. Assured their lips

were sewn, their arms clamped,
I've fallen asleep to the rhythm
of hummed rosaries. My grandfather,

choosing to die on New Year's Day.
His wife, big-boned and stubborn,
paralyzed for fifteen years,

bedridden five, decaying three,
gangrene growing on her back
like some warm carnivorous herb.

An uncle who never spoke a word
until the week he died, insane,
babbling the poison of his liver.

※   ※   ※

I've slept above the dead enough.
Whole generations of a tribe. Still,
in the middle of the night, I hear

the prayers of the living and the dead,
a crescendo through the floorboards,
filling my room like an ancestral chorus:

*Que les âmes des défunts reposent
en paix par la miséricorde
de Dieu.* They have burned

the seams of their eyes, chewed
the nylon cord threaded through
their lips. They have cast off

their clamps. They stand at my
bedside every night moaning my name
off endless strings of beads, burning.

She plants a growing kiss on my forehead.
With her green hand, moist as moss
and wide as my skull, forever free,

she strokes my back and thigh.

To My Brother

You'd think there was no end to this
tribe. They set out and multiplied
as if survival of their species

depended on the acid of their sperm.
Now, in the middle of the night,
they call us to come bury their dead.

So we make that black pilgrimage
back to Lisbon to slide one more
familiar corpse into the holy hillside.

We've buried twelve of them, a dozen
deaths survived, with still a dozen more
or so to live through. The horror

of their deaths and lives lives on
and haunts us: Mandia bent and stunted
by that monster riding her shoulder,

lied into believing she was partly angel;
Blackie drunk before his couple suns
rose every morning of his life, except

the last; and Larry loving various wives,
not one of them his own, his children
strangers to him even when he hemorrhaged;

one Émile lingering for months in
hospital beds infested with leukemia's
piranha, another dropping on the corner

during lunch-hour, gaping blindly back
at the mill hands watching our father
take him in his arms and whisper the act

of contrition to his soulless head.
Time and time again I resurrect them.
They gather in my head, eat, drink and

sing, celebrating their own wakes,
prolonging our interminable deaths.
But each time I return from burying one

of them, all the way back home from
Lisbon I can feel unremembered and
unknown parts of me vanish in the dark

and exhausted silence behind me.
They die, Normand, they die.
And, dying, they kill our only history.

To My Aunt

All through your life
        they lied to you. They said
                a baby-sitter dropped you

and never told your
        mother. They never could
                admit that you were crippled,

born deformed, your shoulder
        jutting out into the blade
                of a stunted wing. Therefore,

they said, you could never
        lead a normal life, and,
                therefore, you never did.

The mutant of our crippled
        wills and hearts, you played
                tribal nurse and clown,

the fool of our cruelty and needs.
        I don't think you ever knew.
                Today we buried you.

No. You were even spared
        that simple fact: ice sealed
                the ground, a clenched and final

pack of lies. But you
        are dead, and, dead, leave
                me obsessed by that hump

and bright lie on your back.
　　　　After they pronounced you
　　　　　　　dead, drained your blood

out of your veins, and dressed
　　　　you like a helpless child,
　　　　　　　was it impossible for them

to close that cage? Did
　　　　your arms, furious, push back
　　　　　　　the leaded lid? Did they raise

you, then, turn you over
　　　　and with a hammer gently
　　　　　　　crack the cartilage of your wing?

Poor dead thing,
　　　　we should have told you all
　　　　　　　along that you were only partly

human. Then, perhaps,
　　　　neither girl nor angel,
　　　　　　　that one thrust of yours

bandaged by your skin,
　　　　with its invisible burning
　　　　　　　mate, might have grown, grown

larger than your frame.
　　　　Before we'd had a chance
　　　　　　　to break that wild wish

riding on your back,
　　　　you could have winged
　　　　　　　yourself away from our lies.

Instead, what you were
        and always will be, now
                always will be trapped

inside the mausoleum
        of our fabricated memory
                until they bury all of us.

But tonight, before
        the ground has thawed, before
                they stuff you in its mouth

rigid as an owl
        at dawn, let me open up
                your cage; let me touch

both sides of your wounded
        back; let me heal you.
                Oh, with the new moon

cracking on the snow
        and all your sisters
                chained to their dying

husbands, sleeping,
        let me show you now
                the truth about yourself.

Just once, *believe*
        the light you feel
                trembling behind you.

Let that inhuman
        power carry you. *Do*
                it. Try. Slowly now,

easy. Rise, yes.
More. Oh, yes. Now
hover. Soar. Fly! Fly!

In the Sleep of Fathers

A mist rose from the river and hovered
in the air, a heavy slab of granite.
Tongues of satin ribbons flapped *Father,*

Father, Husband, Brother from the wreaths
and baskets of dyed flowers on the rented
artificial turf, while your casket quivered

on the tiny elevator that goes down for-
ever. An ancient woman watering her rock
garden in the rain, the priest sprinkled

holy water over you and intoned that last
incantation for the dead's longer-lasting
life, for the deeper sleep of fathers.

The night before, when all your relatives
and friends had left, your sons and daughters
lingered in the mortuary with our mother.

We plucked flowers from the bank that rose
around your bier, a mad farmer's garden
cultivated on the face of some slate cliff,

and laid them as ourselves on your steady
chest, in your hands already grafted
to your ribs. My brother held you in his

outstretched arms, the son he never had,
and begged you to be born again, while we
held each other as we never would again.

Then it was over. Your brothers, sisters,
friends walked back to their cars and slowly
drove off through the cemetery ruled by

our family name. Our wives flanked our mother.
And the undertaker pulled back that blanket
of damp roses children buy to warm their dead.

My brother and I broke two sprigs of ever-
green and placed them just above your mouth.
We knelt and kissed your sealed, implacable

pod one last time. With our knees and feet
still wet with that rich earth surrounding
you as you root yourself deeper, sturdier

in this ground we walk on, in our dreams
we tend to our own families. No longer
sons, we work, we sleep in the sleep of fathers.

Prisoners

I wait until my wife and daughter have survived
the hope of nightmares I can never satisfy.
I wait until the quick-freeze traffic of shifts stops
and factory workers weave to work or home as you did,
until the hot screech of tires has turned cold and mute
in two-car garages under sleek and impotent creatures
serene as saints becoming extinct....

I wait until bars close and my students, higher on
nine months of terrifying freedom from their fathers
than on grass, have fallen into one another's arms.

Father, I wait until that blue, blue moment between
pitch night and milk light when I can almost hear you
whistling those melodies you invented for yourself,
that slow time holding light back, back,
when you were alone and slowly drank your coffee
near the hot woodstove in our small kitchen in Lisbon
in winter, as much at peace as you may be now,
because you wanted it that way. I wait. And when
your presence fills this room with that calm
I slept in as a boy, assuring me I am your son
again, I know it's time to go back to your grave.

Your headstone penetrates the half-light of this
granite sky, but it's no wider than a common cot.
I stretch my heavy body over yours until
the ribs' pressure is returned. I could fall asleep
here. Instead, the hands you gave me gently trace
the small and fragile contours of your shoulders
and your hips. And when I've discovered precisely
where you are, I speak to you — those few words
I've unburied for so few, just to bury them again.

The ground begins to heave, slowly; grass tongues
my ear, a language of love no one understands or
wants to. In the mist rising from the brown river, I can
hear the wide white mouths of the many dead I've loved
breathe a single breath that trembles all to silence.
But *Son. I love you. I forgive you your sins.*
are still prisoners inside your mouth.

Before the sun can touch me, before all those workers'
desperate eyes open, traffic begins again, and my family
discovers I am gone, before I walk back into their light
— with my body still in the furrow it has plowed,
I plant the only seed a guilty firstborn son can
sow, Father, to make us live forever.

The Nameless Garden

I built bonfires of brandy
in my mouth and eyes just
to melt the snow falling
on your lips, the forests
of frost rooted in your hazel
eyes under their closed lids.

In every muscle that I have
I erected dikes of whiskey
to dam the water that might
rise out of you or touch you,
touch, then flood you, rampage
each square inch of you.

I froze my brain with gin
to quench the blazing sun
before it burned your small
bald head, before humidity
sucked a thin eternal moss
out of your wide forehead.

Now maples burn, a gold
fire that doesn't consume;
a softer multicolored flame
spurts from the backs and wings
of pheasants in our field where,
safe from hunters, they can mate

near the thin and silent stream
that gradually stops and is
transformed into a brilliant path
of ice back through the woods —

at peace in a necessary sleep —
to an oasis of silence the purest

white, a garden where no creature,
where nothing, ever lives or dies,
a nameless place my own sleeping
genes remember and long for, long.
Father, I've tried to kill myself
for years to save you from your death.

Once again days shorten, darkness
comes more easily and welcomed. If
I could, I would fly back to Lisbon,
mark off the precise dimensions of
your grave, resurrect your coffin,
pry it open with my own bare hands,

press my mouth against your mouth,
my wrists against your wrists, and
give you back your breath and blood.
But I can't survive us both for long.
In the wilderness you've entered never
to return, offer yourself up to water

that will gently wash your bones until
they're clean and white and free of
life, until the blinding framework of
your body *is* that nameless garden where
all streams converge, where frost and sun
are one, and where you and I, my Father,

finally can be together and at peace.

Figures in a Stranger's Dream

The day you knew your father would give up
his farm in Canada and pack the nine
kids in a hired car to Maine, where his

seven sons could get jobs in the wool
and cotton mills (maybe work a small farm
on the side), you slipped out your window

late at night and stole down to the pasture
where, over tender mounds of grass in their
green fire, spring's cold moonlight hovered

like the dreamt-of echo of an absent snow.
You tore your nightgown off, let fall your hair
until it flowed, a fountain's shimmering

scrim around you, then, with a dancer's breath-
less leap, you straddled your Pa's old and docile
bull, spurred him with your naked heels and,

in a single ring of light, a sphere of
brilliant, pure, accelerating thrust
that fused your porcelain limbs with that

aging creature's sheer brute bulk, you rode him,
rode and rode him, until dawn broke bloodred
under him, until the bull collapsed, until

your brothers came to lift your wet, exhausted
body off its haunches, wrap you in a blanket,
and carry you back to your bedroom in

a wordless covenant that would almost
outlast your lifetime and our own —
as if you had never lived that night, except

as figures in a stranger's dream.
                                        Old woman,
no one's ever known the contours of your
dreams, the figures roaming at their centers.

You spent most your life nursing your father,
as his mouth and eyes filled with greater blank,
and your paralyzed, undying mother,

who fertilized the furrows of her bed
for years with the refuse of her own
decaying flesh until she seemed to root,

a ferocious houseplant feeding on
the breath of unmarried daughters. Breathless
with asthma, you spent nights by your bedroom

window crumbling your beads, novenas'
herbicides ravishing your tongue while
more moonlight than your young heart could

absorb in hope of sleep began to flood
the field, foam and fleece and tide, until
the current in the knots of barbed wire

crackled blue, precise and absolute —
even on the night that old woman died,
your name filling her mouth with her last breath.

And you mothered your unmarried brothers
like three farmers' loyal wives: cooking
as many as nine meals a day, cleaning,

hanging their washed underwear and pants
to dry on winter mornings when the cold
snapped at your fingers with the vengeance of

your mother's gangrene. You put them to bed
when they came home drunk after one more night
with the bovine wives of friends and strangers.

And you buried each of them, one by one,
in that overcrowded family plot
where your name was already branded

in a slab of granite. You sold the farm,
equipment, furniture, your brothers'
handmade tool-chests, mother's linen, crystal

wedding gifts. For days you burned photographs,
love letters, postcards from honeymoons you
never had — anything that would light up the sky.

The last survivor, now the whole history
of the clan, from your great-grandmothers' names
to the glorious fury at the heart of

an unreaped field in moonlight, burgeons
inside their collapsing chests as you live
out your days in a three-room apartment

that shelves on the parish cemetery where
from your bedroom window you can see snow
fall, the disintegrating petals of lost passion.

Tonight your cragged and ancient face is
a worn, familiar planet in slow orbit
above the family pasture where the cattle

of your dreams and mine gently graze a sparser
winter grass. And before your name breaks out,
blooms on the far horizon, obliterates

this small patch of moonlight I cultivate
just by dint of my own breath and hand
as a farmer's son should do, I plumb

a history I have learned, hunch my shoulders,
wish muscles I have never had, flare
my nostrils, call down one last dream of

a young and porcelain woman,
                                        Aurora,
sleepwalking in a scrim of hair,
and offer you my eager, docile back.

To My Sister

All day the dead are still.
Anchored in the hangar
in the hillside, their arms

clamped wings of wild
prehistoric birds
at the bottom of the sea,

they rock, gentle with the tides,
the tilting earth and winds,
invisible and benign.

It's at night, when nothing
living moves, when mirrors
open up like caskets

that they start. Whining,
trembling, the fuel of
their familiar fury burns,

and they sail, horizontal,
moving at inhuman speeds.
Their feet propel them.

The whole armada of our
clan invades my lawn
churning like the sea,

the few fathoms of air
I claim as mine. Huge
and deadly destroyers,

they violate my skull's
sovereignty I've fought for
for years. Anne, tonight

they've come to fight and win.
I feel the infrared blinking
of their eyes in mine. And,

ready to launch the torpedoes
of their hearts, the humming
of their spinning ribs tracks

my heart beat, beat by beat.

The Wait

I've been expecting you
all night. All night
my table's circle of
bright light trembled,
the corners of the room
blasted off into space.
I've been waiting for
you to be there across
from me, finishing some-
thing you'd started to
say so many years ago,
perhaps beginning what
you never could before.

All night I've waited
for you to come from
that other realm, a moth
consummating your mission,
eyes red with an inhuman
fire flashing, flashing
a code it could take me
a lifetime to decipher,
or just to stand there
at the dim edge of my eye,
the fern's fine fronds,
a green shimmer of breath.

Watching me without one
word would be enough.
Because, brother, father,
final lover, all night
I've been expecting you.
Now dawn hammers joists

back into place, blots out
my lamplight. Calm seeps
in. You won't come and,
if you do, I won't be here.

The Moth

In summer here the moths are big as birds.
No one dares go out at night. They used to
stampede cattle, once; now, late at night, they
dive at the last window lit with the frenzy
of light. Children think they feed on them.
Wanting to warn me, my neighbors say: Out there,
in the center of the dead grove of pines, silent
as a cocoon, one of them's bigger than a man.
He's the father of them all, a kind of Lord & God.

And I've waited for him all summer long.
I've stayed awake until dawn looking for him.
One night his eyes will burn, a fallen angel
at my window. His bright wings will tremble
with the promise of another ecstasy and peace.
The glass will melt. He'll hover vertically,
as if forever. But finally, with his thin lips
against my throat, he'll wrap me in the cool
darkness of his wings, space will disappear,
and I will rise again in that white silence
my brothers and neighbors have always feared.

Fireflies

The sweet smell of wild straw-
berries and hay crushed in my
back, thirty years ago I'd fall
asleep with flashes of fireflies
by my bed, a whole tribe of eyes,
the guardian angels of my genes.

Now it's winter where I live
and each breath I take is rye.
Curled up in my percale pasture,
a fetus praying the terrible
dark for sleep, the luciferin
light of their deaths and lives
still blinks on and off inside
the glass of my balding head.

The glow of my grandmother's
gangrene. My godmother's cells
scorched whiter and whiter in her
memory. Cancer's blood-blue
ember in my father's throat.
I wait for that mysterious fuel
to exhaust itself, the almost
inaudible click of one worm's
corpse falling into final dark.

They won't burn out. They will
not die. They flash and flash,
a borealis in my clenched eyes.
They carve their shadows in this
glass growing thinner every night.
A spark's ignited at the center of
my skull. Soon we'll all be free.

The First Day

for Peter Fiore

At least twenty million and often as many as five
hundred million sperm cells should be present in
a single ejaculation.

G.L. FLANAGAN

Under the proper clinical conditions
I could have populated planets,
made Solomon look impotent
and the Seven Tribes of Judah sound
like the litter of a pampered bitch.

Patristic coverage would've been fantastic:
"On the first day, with his first ejaculation,
he begat five hundred million sons
and daughters. On the first day
with his third ejaculation he begat
three hundred million sons and daughters.
On the first day, with his fifth ejaculation,
he begat…" On and on, riding inspired
rhythms until the last ejecta left me
exhausted and expiring like some ancient
fish at the mouth of a high and spring-
fed river in the wildest wood.

High in the Maine woods instead,
on those hot days, while blue-
berries bled on my back, while
the screech of cicadas rose
to an inhuman pitch, while fish
suffocated in the pond, hounds
howling at the moon, lost, and
while the sun annihilated
galaxies spinning in my skull,

as I moaned   they came
dying on the desert
of my chest   they came
dying on my burning
rocks   dying
they   came
in the oven of my hand.

Oh   my   sons
     and   daughters
I   called   you
to   be   food   for
the   worms   of   this   earth.

On Our Unborn Child

to Basilike

Cleopatra in the guise
    of Theda Bara plastered
        on our bathroom wall

has immortal longings
    every night about three
        in the morning, and with thick

papery flutters, rustling
    wings on the angel of death,
        collapses in the bathtub.

The Corvair's exhaust pipe
    and muffler have succumbed
        to road salt and to rust,

fallen, and every morning
    as we roar to class,
        monoxidal fumes ride

the rush of cold air
    from the heater, tempting
        us to sleep and dreams sturdier

than those we've awakened
    from to go to every day,
        every morning, every night.

And poor Jack, the rare
    late-autumn days have knit
        his jaw into thick clumps

of orange skin wilting; rot
blisters on his lower lip;
a gray moss beards his chin.

A month ago he was our own
St. Elmo's fire smiling
two-toothed above the lawn,

as we sailed through another
year of strangers in this old hulk.
Tonight the dull fire of his mouth,

hissing as it burns
the soft pulp of his head,
might be the foolish glow

of gas above a marsh or graveyard.
Jack should be in bed,
his head hollowing a pillow.

Jack looks like my grandmother,
her face caving in to gangrene
eating away inside her head

until she died, mouth
open, an enormous foul hole
behind her lipless grin.

And me, Love, Christ, look.
My pores are swollen: beads
of skin cluster on my chin.

They tell me as I get older
I look more like my grandmother
when I smile. Last night I dreamed

she was sleeping beside you.
　　　She wore Jack's hollow head.
　　　　　　Love, I dreamt I was dead.

Look, Love, while you bloom,
　　　the rest of us decay.
　　　　　　Flies buzz around our eyes.

But I'll have the muffler fixed.
　　　Tomorrow I'll dispose of poor Jack's head.
　　　　　　Let the dying bury the dead.

And you, bloom to one
　　　inside you, one who'll live
　　　　　　my grandmother's name,

my father's name and mine,
　　　a child born at Christmas time,
　　　　　　my seed thriving in you, my slime.

In Advent

for Basilike and Daphne

I

According to our calculations
You were expected long ago.

But still you crouch inside
The cage of your mother's veins,

A creature conceived by another
Creature, winged, sacred, secret.

Others like you have been known
To be too early or too late

And we've been always unprepared.
Advent is our only season.

II

Although this winter night's
Ablaze with shafts of lightning

Edged with mauve and echoes
With the roar of thunder

Like the sea crashing down
On a pursuing army,

What can I do? I can't
Deliver you from your captivity.

And once you've escaped
Into this wilderness

Where every night promises
No more than itself, and you

Have shown a measure of good
Will and a capacity to survive,

I'll be of no greater use
To you. I'm no one's delegate.

My laws are my own, shifting
With the sand I walk on.

I can't legislate for you, and
I won't promise you the land

When I can't promise you today.
I'm amazed by every morning:

I sing and dance, even for the sand,
And praise the burning at my feet.

Child, I am a desert creature,
One of a nomad tribe, accustomed

To betrayal by the mirage of need.
But this is what I chose,

With David, Ruth and Paul: exile,
The terror of the constant sun

Obliterating every trace of prayer
And law from the ghetto of my tongue;

The wind demolishing my words,
Dust seeping into my bones;

Rats spying on my every wish,
Attacking every hope every night.

But this is what I chose,
Rather than complicity with prelates

Who, with a Nazi zeal,
Will execute their own,

Make candles of their fat,
Thuribles of their skulls,

Stoles of their embroidered skin —
Sacramentals for their rituals

To preserve the sweet, rich blood
Of their infected race.

I am obsessed by the memory
Of murdered friends.

In dreams I finger their bones
Like beads, burning.

Their ashes stir and glow
In the reliquaries of my eyes.

If you choose to search for
Still another atmosphere, Child,

You'll have to find your own
Way out. I can't deliver you.

III
You'd think yours is going to be
Another virgin birth, redemption

In some Iowan farmer's stable,
Cornhusks for your cradle,

Attended by the Aga Khan,
Pope Paul and Martin Luther

King. I see them kneeling,
Wise in the wealth of silos,

Silent, round and solid
As the towers of old temples;

TV antennas, stainless-steel
Angels on rooftops transmitting

Heavenly messages to farmhands
Dozing on the frozen hillsides.

IV

Where do we go from here?
What frontier, sea or galaxy

Will we have to cross disguised
As night creatures, warming our hands

To the thin embers of twigs,
Feeding on cactus and raw fish,

Slaking our throats with salt
Water or juices of wild locust,

Like fugitives to find asylum?
What drunken governor, anxious

For safety of his state,
Will sign your execution?

How many children will soldiers
Slaughter so you can live?

In what desert, jungle, city street
Or campus will you wage the war

The rest of us keep losing
Every day? Each day conquered.

What friend will betray you
To the priests? What priest

Will sell you to the state?
Child, we're all Black, all Jews.

Every minute is an exodus.
Hours roar like cattle trains.

Each day is an oven.
Our skulls wish for the bullet's kiss.

How many governors and good
Citizens will be saved by law and order?

Will I live because you died?

5

Child, I don't know
If you've been fathered

To be a prince of peace
Or criminal. My name

In the official census
Is Joseph. All I can

Do is build a bed
And roof for you, supply

You with my name,
My blood and race,

My species; then, season
After season, wait.

December 9, 1966

To Daphne on the Third and Fourth Days of Her Life

You live and breathe
in a simulated atmosphere,
rarefied, behind a shield

of glass, protected
from our infected
air, your natural

habitat. I visit you,
a stranger to your needs,
touch and speak to you

with the help of media:
an intercom and nurse,
sterilized and masked,

disinfected intercessor.
Contaminated, dangerous,
I am still your father.

I'm your originator.
For centuries it seems
I watched you make

your way into my world.
With my ear pressed
against the wall of skin

that separated us,
I heard you swim from side
to side, primeval, precious

fish in my wife's sea.
I later felt the contours
of your spine, the probing

of your foot or fist,
child, still not quite
born, still not quite human

enough to breathe my air.

II

Today I bring you home.
I am prepared to sterilize
utensils, bottles, nipples,

boil the water you will drink.
If needs be, I'll sterilize
the sterilizer, eradicate

a whole race of bacteria
with a Hitler hysteria.
I'll be antiseptic.

But I can't purify
this air you'll breathe.
The air, the air — it is

diseased. It germinates
despair. It can't be
filtered of the shrieks

of burning tongues, throats
melting in Hiroshima,
Auschwitz or in Vietnam.

Each day and night smells
of dead burnt fat and hair.
Each breath will grease

your lungs, atomic soot
will plug your throat.
What artificial respiration

can I provide for you?
Poems are my iron lungs.
These weird contraptions

pump and pump my chest,
pressure me to survive
each day. I live in

their chambers and praise
the current that makes
them work. But I

can't make a poem
strong enough to help
us both. No poet can

or will. Someday you
may discover or invent
your own machinery

to survive. Until then,
we're still divided
by that wall that separates

the living from the dead.

Begin Again

I

An aging migratory creature
    whose survival hinges on a yearly trek
        back to its species' native breeding grounds,

I have returned to this small coastal town
    in Maine where everything decays too soon
        and nothing ever dies quite soon enough.

Here, each day is another failure
    of another lifetime deposited across
        the foreign landscape of forgotten dreams.

Here, in the haze of oaks and elms ablaze
    with no more than a residue
        of oxygen and sap, cracked and peeling

plaster casts of dwarfed deer graze on blistered
    grass; whiter each day, winter brooding
        in their intricately beautiful and

brainless skulls, they inch toward old abandoned
    porches that will never be consoled,
        toward the char, the sudden frost, the utter

desolation at the heart of every
    open eye and palm. I was born here.
        My father's buried here, his father,

mother, and his brothers, all aligned
    precisely in the family plot according
        to the schema of our tree, and they root

themselves and me more deeply in this
        rocky ground than when we tried to work
                it for a living. Tonight I sit alone,

absorbing darkness resonating with
        the ancient music of the sea, the echo
                of our common womb, while far above that

distant, bare Atlantic field the faces
        of my family bloom, a brilliant tribal
                constellation ruling in a starless sky.

                              II

My wife and daughter are asleep, their bodies
        glowing with the sunlight they've absorbed all
                day, refracting their excess of light back

into the dark that barely touches them.
        Each day these two women grow into more
                beautiful reflections of each other,

as their limbs enclose the day's last rays
        of sun, petals of dark flowers that are
                still strangers in this motherland of memory.

I walk into the light of their deep sleep
        and breathe the nimbus of their dream:
                let these lovely women sleep; let them wake

refreshed; let them slowly stretch themselves
        open to the sun again, dawn clinging
                to their bodies' down, a brilliant dew;

and let them never get attached enough
        to this coastal land to long to live here
                as wild columbines flowering among the rocks.

Their history is unfolding in another
        land, a far more gentle future place
                where I may join them when my work is done.

Alone again, I inhale the dark,
        an ancient lover's breath: at last,
                tonight, brittle seeds of light begin

to orbit in my ankles, in my wrists,
        sail the uncharted inner space of my bones,
                blossom with a meteoric fury in my mouth.

                        III
Like flocks of gulls around a fishing boat
        when the men are cleaning the day's catch,
                dumping heads and innards overboard, blood

blooming in the heaving sea, petals
        of ferocious underwater flowers,
                or as if my name were the intaglio

at the prehistoric center of
        each atom constituting their genetic
                molecules, tonight again moths swarm

at my window, perch on the precise,
        geometric lacing of the screen,
                a gleaming membrane separating

need from mere ambition, a film between
        blank memory and the future's incandescence.
                You know the myth of moths among the folk

here: they say they're souls of dead lovers,
        relatives and friends granted a reprieve
                from darkness one night every year to hunt

the living, offer you the secrets
of the dead imprinted on their wings,
flashing in their desperate eyes, in exchange

for particles of light swimming in your
blood: glimpses of a future where the memory
of sons is the fathers' fullness of desire.

And if you can decipher that rare code,
they will hunt you down again next year.
This is my fortieth. Those light-thirsty

angels have fished my veins a decade.
I know more about the dead than I'll
ever care to know: they cultivate

the mushrooms of their cryptic spores in
the damp cellars of my chest where darkness
rules and has been reigning far too long.

Knowing what was sown, what little ever
flourished, what the fruit of that ambitious
future surely is, finally the time

has come to cut myself off from a tree
I never planted, to uproot myself
from this unyielding land, to strip away

dead branches with those old nests and cocoons
abandoned long ago, to set all that
debris ablaze, and to begin again.

IV

The lamp erects a fence and stakes out
a small pasture of pure light on the edge
of one more day that would collapse beneath

the weight of so much darkness at its
        center. Wild with the very smell of light,
                a galaxy of moths — their wild faces as

familiar as my own, wings delicate
        and decorated, tiny heirloom doilies
                embroidered by a tribe of lonely women —

gather like a herd of famished deer
        after weeks of bitter winter, come
                to graze the orchard of my palms, gardens

of my two bare wrists. One by one I let
        them in, hold them in my outstretched hand
                with a cautious tenderness reserved

for the very fragile, the most precious
        of exotic flowers; one by one I speak
                their names with love, as if each were my own:

Alfred, Alphonse, Mélanie, Aurora,
        Azarie, Rose, Napoleon, Ovila, Émile,
                Florida, Evangeline, William, Laurier…

and one by one, in a measure of more
        light than they have ever known, without
                any compromise, for a moment that will

last them an eternity, they breathe,
        they rise, they suddenly disintegrate
                in the acetylene of my loving breath.

                        v

My table's littered with small stars of ash,
        a burnt-out nebula that would never
                fill the cupped hand of my sleeping daughter.

Before dawn breaks above the bay, before
    my wife and daughter wake, never knowing
        that the constellation of those ruling

planets rooted in the vast Atlantic sky
    vanished as they slept, with my night's
        work done, like a factory hand after one

more eight-hour shift, I wash the oil
    and soot clinging to my hands and face and
        stretch out in the glowing garden of our bed.

Dawn: a full and brilliant sun rises
    from the sea, slowly hauling soundless
        echoes of itself from deep within

our lungs, reverberating in our
    open mouths and leaping from our lips,
        as bright sonatas bloom inside our brains.

☒ ☒ ☒ ☒ ☒ ☒ ☒

PART II

Lament in Spring

At the heart of that thick grove of pines
beyond the lawn, at high noon
today I found a tiny and unearthly-
pale blue egg, more fragile

than an eye, that had fallen from a nest
and floated in a blinding
pool of spring-fed sunlight — the fetus of
a rare and undiscovered

starfish. With my fingers interlaced
into a cautious net, I
slowly scooped it closer to my face
just to wonder at its color,

just to thrill over such a brittle shell.
But when I breathed a deeper
breath of awe, that small egg shattered
in my open palm — and once

again I felt the wing of madness brush
my temple with the fury
brooding in the ova of all fragile
things for centuries. My friend,

in this sometimes gentle world where we must
give and give and give just
to survive, there are things that do and
always will shatter merely

from the brunt of awesome human breath.
We have been two of them.

Tonight, as I prepare for sleep, I stand
before the mirror, shimmering

with its antique silvered weight: my naked
body glows its own pale hue
and once again I am as vulnerable
as any man-made thing.

Stars plummet into distant seas, the wind
gusts, and one tiny feather,
clinging to my thinning hair, wildly flutters
inches from my pale blue eye.

Against Spring

My nose starts to itch:
a jonquil full of pollen
with a bee buzzing in it,
worming up into my brain
and out into the sunlight.

I become myopic.
The forsythia bush
outside our window is
a constellation of suns.

Rising from their own
reflections, fountains
springing from the dark
cool caverns in the earth,
willows by the river, love,
are angels, wild angels
on the muddy riverbank,
wholly still and silent,
the palest green, waiting.

Today the wind. God,
what a wind weeding out
my hair, the soft brown
stalks of last year's
zinnias left to frost
and snow, and rooting
out dead limbs
of trees that crashed
around me and exploded
shrapnel of their pulp
against my legs and chest.

It's spring again.
The infected cornea of ice
has fallen from our windows,
and raw light lacerates
the nerves and muscles
of our rooms. You air out
a winter's worth of blankets.
My seed seeds the lawn.

And at the private center
of your eyes where I have
never been, delicate, white
and fragrant as a May flower,
a love begins to bloom, wild
in the woods of your loneliness,
and it is not for me. Oh,
love, I am afraid of spring.

Script Prospectus

to his wife

I'm scared out of my mind,
scared to death. Looney
tunes run on inside my head,

scores for mad scenarios.
Any day now I'll be waiting
for a subway and someone

gone berserk on smog will
shove me: neck and ankles
sizzling sparks; a train

will dismember me. Any day
on my way to talk to my
conscientious class on

the ways and means of poetry,
another Whitman boy, obsessed
by his belief in words, will seize

me in his sight and, balanced
on a ledge or trembling
by a window, will blast my head

wide open. Darling, any day
now I'll make love to you
and in the thrashing of your

frenzy you'll slip a knife
into my spine, or I'll come
home and toss our baby into

our roaring hearth. I'll drink
from a bubbler chilled
by a live wire meant for that

girl behind me and immolate
myself by accident, with cal-
culated satisfaction jab

a jugular while shaving, lose
my shirt at craps, or step
into an open elevator shaft.

Darling, I'm not paranoid.
But as if invisible agents
of some unsuspected enemy

emptied vials of secret
formula into our reservoirs,
sprayed our orchards while

we slept, these days even
the most gentle of our friends
and citizens blink, shiver,

and are monsters, products
and victims of a supreme
mad scientist. Young men mix

a pig's blood with their own
and pour it into filing
cabinets. Others make huge

bonfires of their bones and hair.
A mother carves the heart out
of her four-year-old son's chest

and makes a sacred menorah
of his ribs. A couple
vaccinate their children

with insecticide to collect
double indemnity. And, Lord,
these aren't even metaphors

or scripts for class-B flicks.
But the daily news. Something's
wrong. I must write my congress-

man, demand a national inquiry.
The only sanctuary left is
exile or asylum. And hell, no,

darling, I won't go. Still
until this mystery is solved,
until we've discovered what

inhuman agent is responsible
for all of this, every time
I hear someone running hard

behind me or laughing loud
and invisible, I'll be scared.
And every night inside my head

the same old horror show: any
day some stranger, relative or
friend will kill me. Or you will.

Science

Love, I've spent nights down
in the cellar poring
over letters from your
past-and-younger lovers,
a monk becoming
blind and impotent.
I've parsed their sentences
and made meticulous charts
of the geneal-
logy of my ignorance
for the smallest clue
to rediscover you.

Every night I've heard you
moan and toss above me,
some wild saint asleep
alone in our bed,
scratching at the black thighs
of the air, the woolen
backs of blankets, while I
itched to be torn open
like a goat or bread.
At dawn I have come back
upstairs, my eyes ringed
as a voyeur's, to crawl
back into bed, still dumb,
and curl up against you.

I've learned nothing in four
years. Each day I un-
learn more. You move about
the house quiet as
calculus, a foreign

language my tongue will
never master. Even
when I'm deep inside you,
probing for my own dark
center, you remain
an aboriginal
superstition. You are
impenetrable.

You fall asleep, dream
and whisper the names
of wiser men who
solved that riddle that
you harbor like some
undiscovered and essential
element or atom.

Song in Spring

to Basilike

The lilies of the valley that I picked
for you faded in one day.
But all day those white and tiny bells
poured the breathless music

of their odor in our room and made us
dizzy, as in dance or
as — on a brilliant morning in the Alps
while canton bells intone

the Angelus — lovers who have tasted
death. Tonight their ecstatic
perfume's music echoes still in consort
with Mozart's mild sonatas,

and the crystal vase that was their brilliant
sepulchre for one rare day
is still ringing with so much of their
memory beyond the pitch

of sound, it threatens to disintegrate
into a dust of light
and root itself in our flowerbed.
By morning that vase will be

empty glass again; we will have forgotten
flowers that so briefly graced
our lives among demands of daily love
and work: these words with wills

of steel I labor to anneal into
a tougher tongue; the fired

metal which you forge toward that sound of
a pure language all your own;

this marriage that continues to refuse
to break under the brunt
of habit and assumption. But tonight,
let the dream of these frail, white

lilies speak: Love, if death must touch our tongues
when we are in full bloom,
then let our memory survive that grave
business in our music's wild perfume.

September 1, 1979

to Basilike

Scientists have noted that over the centuries sharks
have been growing longer and thinner.

All day the bay has blazed a blue so blue
and so essential only to itself
it seemed about to surface and assume
a substance all its own. Shafts of sunlight

swam and darted through the tide, a school
of ancient sharks limned for sleepless centuries
by the sea, by instinct's will, and come
to our bay by choice where, one by one,

they made their final, everlasting leap
from fish to pure and elemental light.
Outside our bedroom window, mushrooms
have been growing blindly in the dark,

in the relentless rain of all-night storms
for days. Tonight they are a dozen suns
in orbit on the forest floor, their centers
palpable and orange August moons rising

from uncharted seas, spreading halos
of their spores around them on the intri-
cately delicate green face of moss, and
rooting in the sleepless blue still moored

in our eyes. If only for a moment
as deceptive as dead stars, on these rare
days we can believe we too are dreams
of this world that we feel slowly spinning

in its inner orbit toward what it dreams
to be. In our shadows lying at our feet,
the echoes of a hope we thought we had
abandoned long ago, our longings suddenly

ignite by instinct, mushroom into will,
fill us with a blinding glimpse of our own
rare and elemental selves leaping toward
that more essential, that more lasting

substance we must be, blazing like a pure
and newborn planet long before its light
is seen, shedding nebulaes of bright
particles of dust rooting in the dead's

wide and sleep-blind eyes.
                              Before I go to bed,
I raise the electromagnetic mirrors of my hands
toward those stars where none of this earth's days
has reached its end, and I re-call today

before it dawns again, light-years from now,
in a dimension other than our own.
As if to bless the cosmos for this one
day's glimpse and gift of what we are,

I kneel and gently cup my hands above
the calm and tender orbs of your closed eyes
still refracting light back into the dark
that barely touches them. My prayer, Love,

isn't to that void beyond the reach of sound.
Instead — before the winter's dark descends,
before breath's tendrils turn to ice and
burgeon in our lungs, before crazed buds

of blood bloom and shatter in the barren
vineyard of our veins — my cupped hands brood
above your eyes until all energy is drained
from them, until your eyelids' luminescence

testifies: in you (and so in me) will dawn,
again and then again, this day when
all day the bay has blazed a blue so blue
and so essential to itself, to me and you,

that once, just once, we surfaced and assumed
this rare and elemental substance all our own.

Testament

And now our bedroom's sealed,
the tomb of Pharaoh
stirring with huge spiders,

reincarnations of ourselves.
Your kiss devours me.
Our bed is an anthill.

With every cave and crevice
of our bodies full of honey,
trembling liquid gold, our

words, the teeth of memory,
begin their work. But our
bones are secret passage-

ways winding down to the center
of the earth where, leaping
up like lava, mysteries

are still unearthed, where love,
an offering left by the living
for the dead, can crystallize.

And there, love, among un-
discovered kings, we will not die.

Cave Dwellers

I've carved a cave in the mountainside.
I've drilled for water, stocked provisions
to last a lifetime. The walls are smooth.
We can live here, love, safe from elements.
We'll invent another love that can't destroy.
We'll make exquisite reproductions of our
selves, immortal on these walls.

                        And when
this sea that can't support us is burned clean,
when the first new creatures crawl from it,
gasping for water, air, more wondrous and more
wild than earth's first couple, they shall see
there were two before them: you and me.

Daughter's Song

Daphne, another day
    of tiny miracles
        as frangible as

daughters in their
    slow, tender blooming
        into strong and lovely

women, ineffable
    epiphanies, revealed
        more by the light

song of their being
    all and only what they
        are than by any telling.

This morning two pale
    mourning doves, like aged
        lovers who have learned

love's longer-lasting
    tongue, coo their
        soft monotone lament,

echoed by the bees
    that pollinate the air
        around this magnolia

with perfume that might
    make younger lovers
        wild with love's anxieties.

In the hemlock near
        my door, a robin's
                nest, as vulnerable

as any shelter
        that a father builds.
                In it: four brilliant

eggs asserting those
        clichés of their blue
                with a loud and brittle

melancholy, as if
        they were being hatched
                in Eden. On my desk

the mushroom that I
        picked two days ago:
                withered, dehydrated,

and now the small
        but labyrinthine
                heart-shaped dead brain

of a unicorn,
        its horn still and
                forever locked in place,

the tip blossomed
        into white lips thick
                with a purer pitch of love,

the ecstasy of speech.
        You see, there are things
                in this often silent human

world a father cannot
        teach his daughter.
                He can only speak them:

Dove. Egg. Mushroom.
        And the fire that I
                built to ward off this

early evening chill
        flares in my eyes again
                as its warm laurel tongues,
                        without song, sing: *Daphne.*

Children in Fog

to M.W.

Ebb tide: a thin fog sails in from the sea
and moors on the Atlantic
coast. Houses vanish, our neighbors on
the beach start to dissolve

and each thin thread of hair on our bodies
turns to white, heavy with
a warm and gentle sea-mist. Suddenly,
we are figures in this land-

scape's dream again, floating in and out
of one another with the heave
of tides and exchanging histories
like breath in lovers' mouths.

In our children's eyes, we are fathers
flying toward the vanished point
of our own history, returning only
in their dreams, as we always

will; and where the sea and the horizon
fuse, they are baby dolphins
leaping out of breakers, stuttering that
music we inhaled, once, long

ago, and hammered into tongues of law.
Neither males nor females of
their species, they still love themselves so much
they are buoyant in this mist,

their wake bright parabolas of light. They swim
toward us so slowly, they could

never reach us in our lifetime or their own.
Michael, they're so substance-

less, they might also dive into our eyes
and nest there deep inside
our brains to resurrect as memories
remembered in another life.

The landscape dreams us into motion;
we dream ourselves leaping from
a brilliant sea; we wake in
an imaginary country,

strangers in these strangers' heavy bodies
white with frost, a music in
our throats as primordial as scrimshaw
replicas of our descendants —

and we drown, only to awaken once
again, here, on the Atlantic
coast, as our children's names soar from our open
mouths until they swim toward us

again and we know they are still safe.
In this haze that has become
as much light as it is water, Michael,
this could be the day when

children of the sea first breathed oxygen
and miraculously walked
on land — or that other, when the offspring
of this earth long for hydrogen

again, unleash its law that will impose
a momentary order
all its own, when, like the other fathers,
we'll come to this coast again

and wait for our bodies' every sinew
to blaze brightly, from within,
for our children's bodies to collapse
around their feet like starfish,

while the music from their vanished mouths
will leap back into the breakers,
back into the throats of dolphins swimming,
slowly swimming in our eyes.

Factory Hands

He comes here every day after his eight-
hour shift, his forearms shining with that
deep and lasting glow of good industrial oil.

Wisps of cotton still cling to his hair;
his body's filaments are spun tight spools
of muscle; the bass whine of the spinning

room reverberates in the porous fibers
of his bones. He strips and swims; he swims
the drone of lubricated gears out of his

system for another day. Spent as a husband,
he rises from the sea, glistening with sea
spray and with salt, stretches on the sand,

offers his exhausted body to the sun. He sleeps.
For minutes that could last the lifetime he
will never live, he breathes bright sunlight.

What impossible ambition, what inhuman lover
sprouts a dream inside his lungs, travels
his veins' entangled vineyard, ripples every

tendon into bloom, writhes and arches his
whole body till he softly moans — as if
an unknown tongue of satisfaction touched

his very center once, and then again? Ahh,
this beautiful young man's body will be
wasted with his dreams long before he wakes,

before he's thirty, sullen, married to some
sullen woman in a weave of mutual betrayals
where the automatic murder of each other

or their kids will be the casual nightmare
of their hopes. And the sea's incessant hum
will vibrate in his inner ear, as all that

elaborate machinery of his life, gone berserk
with useless overuse, spins out of control,
and the last few shreds of love, of all desire,

unravel at his feet on a blazing summer after-
noon, in the middle of some eight-hour shift.

II

I've known this sleeping stranger all my life.
He's one of those young men, their eyes as old
with unrelenting terror as their fathers',

I worked with years ago in the wool and cotton
mills to pay my own way out of my father's
futile dreams. He is my younger brother.

Even to this day, he never has forgiven
me: my bone-white, small and delicate hands;
my unmanly fumbling with machinery;

my working hours weaving tapestries
of sound with no more than the thin strands
of my brain; my passion for escape; my will

never to be some factory hand collapsed
in base exhaustion on any blazing beach
or bed. And in the universe of just

reversals, he is me divining this
young stranger's dream of who *I* just might be.

III

I have come here every day after another
sleepless night, my thighs still wet with
the sweat of lovers — faceless, masterful

mechanics of the body's warp and woof,
its every joint and screw. After having
been worked over by those technicians of

the machineries of pleasure, my every
nerve-end aches with memory still spinning
from its center, a residue of ecstasy

that no lye or Atlantic would wash out.
Glistening with the last few drops of
coconut oil some beautiful young thing

bought me in Hawaii, I begin a new
day's work: the plots, the intrigues, rumors
of the grapevine — no less elusive than

the irreversible burst of those small
veins in the blue arbor of my ankles,
the bubbles of bright blood that refused

to burst in the press of my own stubborn
heart. My friend, my beautiful young brother,
this stranger sleeping next to me, never

could fathom why I come here every day
to offer my own oiled, exhausted body
to the sun, to sleep another lifetime,

pray ultraviolet rays of suns
in still another universe to obliterate
the memory of all human and inhuman

lovers, the bloom and seed of uselessly
abused ambition, before the compli-
cated machinations of my life

grind to a halt and, in the middle of
some blazing summer afternoon, un-
ravel in my brain, my mouth, a tongue,

a language, just one simple human phrase
or word — a weapon gone berserk.
My friend, let our beautiful strange brothers sleep.

Poem on a Photograph of a Young Painter

to K.E.

You stand before your painting
of a soldier's empty shirt that hovers
vertically between the azure
of a stormed Aegean sky, the flesh tones

of a frail imagined beach.
With one hand in your pocket, your full weight
resting on one leg, you wear
your own brilliant white silk shirt, tinged bronze

by your body's olive hue,
your designer's jacket of soft black velour —
the clothes you wore the last time
that I saw you, at home and comfortable

in the old-world splendor
of the Hotel Grande Bretagne in Athens;
but your body has assumed
the same posture as that army tunic

suspended in midair
by the relentless memory of a warm
and wounded presence, still shaped
by the absent contours of the young man's

body it discarded on
a long-deserted battlefield no one's
ever won — and now become
the vestment of a dark and terrifying

angel. In your letter's
broken English, you say you must set your

daily art aside and, soon,
report for your years of service in one

of this world's oldest armies.
Now you must learn the tactics of a more
ancient art: to recognize
the enemy that hides even in a lover's

heart and, without honor,
without guilt, but with the calculated,
mindless gestures of that long-
danced liturgy of war, to kill and to be

killed. My friend, don't look for me
in this poem's loosely measured syllables;
for before you have arrived
at that wordless momentary peace all

art offers to another,
I will have stepped outside of this
ballet of breath, climbed a ladder
of my own making back into that

photograph of you, and leapt
into your painting; and there, in midair,
between the azure bolt
of hopeless sky and the more familiar

human beach, I'll have assumed
that disembodied shirt as if it had
been mine from the beginning,
and I shall hover over

you, unseen, as if, from one
dimension to another, this warm breath
in your hair tonight were mine,
so that other angel cannot leap from

the fabricated realm of art
and with vengeance clamp its dark vestment
of despair around your all too human
body, your all too guileless heart.

Saltimbanques

He was assailed by a sense of wonder for waste.

DAPHNE ATHAS

I

Although summer's barely started, roses
are in bloom; you buy roses
for our small rented house, more red roses
than we have flower vases,
empty bottles for. And you laugh, "Roses
are for lovers!" Your flushed face
repeats and multiplies your lavish gift.

You stand in our villa's door,
ablaze, a reckless angel leaning
on no more than a scaffold
of sheer sunlight, exhaling oxygen
too rarefied for this heart
propped on the blood of others, reconstructed
to endure in that more common
realm where breath is forged into
brutal weapons in the mouths
of lovers. That gift of your love's
extraordinary architecture
would have been extravagant enough
to have sustained me for
at least one lifetime I have never lived.
But since you taught my body
how to love more than I knew it capable
of loving and survive, I
welcome this excess of roses, each bloom
excessive as a human
heart, as unwarranted as our love.

Two strangers magnetized
into each other's time and space by love's
stranger law of gravity,
we've learned the art of mastering the techniques
of our love's complicated
calculations taxing our bodies more
than the more fundamental
mathematics of the marriage bed.

And when we come together
at the pitch of our love's slow, agonized
amazement, every strand in
our tempered brains knows nothing will become
of us and nothing will come
of this love conceived as its own end
from the very start. For what
we do, we do for nothing other than
the simple act of loving,
of being nothing more than all we are,
all we've chosen to become —

just as a troupe of seasoned acrobats,
with no audience in sight,
will rehearse to conquer their contorted
limbs into such precise and
willed submission that in slow and total
unison all the bones
and muscles of their arms and legs, their ankles
and their wrists, begin to stretch,
to bend and arch, then bloom into a
more-than-human and amazing
flower, each limb a petal of the whole,
breathless and suspended in
nothing but the midair of imagination,
of the will to be no more

than just a flower of flesh that lives but
for a moment — seedless, issue-
less, glorious — and all too suddenly
or slowly sheds its all-
too-human petals of just ordinary
men and women back onto
the stage, back into the street, back into
the sidereal common
denominator of their separate lives.

III

See how those roses already
have begun to fade, as if exhausted
by the very will to bloom
trapped in their heartless seeds, which none has learned
to master, which still masters
them and spins them still atop their stems
to blossom once again far
above themselves, like an imagined corps
of high-wire *saltimbanques*
forever leaping, weightless, on the scaffold
of pure space. Our water will
prolong their death, the slow decomposition
of their perfect selves as one
more shape of what this earth has dreamed to be
in its decaying orbit
of the sun, calculated by the vast
imagination of millennia.
Soon they'll shed their petals, embers of
the tongues of memory burning
themselves out forever in their endless fall
back into the earth, the ground,
the forge of their imagined selves and ours.

The Singers

With their arms flung over one another's shoulders,
    breasts and backbones resonating as they touch,
        these six young men are sculptured by the music

that they sing. Originating in the solid bar
    of marble that's their ground, a silence surging
        toward the shape of sound, it rises into feet

and ankles, forms and tempers the thick muscles
    in their calves and thighs, accentuates the sloping
        contours of their hips. The wish for music fuses

with the growing hum of breath inside their chests;
    doubles; strains their ribs until they vibrate
        at a breaking point; arcs the taut fibrillae

ringing in their spinal cords, the tendons
    in their necks; and elevates their faces, eyes
        and opened mouths to the pitch of speechless

agonizing joy — until, precisely when the music
    that they are would be transformed into one clear
        reverberating note sustained as long as marble

might endure, it turns upon itself; plunges
    back into their throats; and fills their bodies
        once again until they seem one step removed

from leaping like a line of dancers out of stone;
    until these six young singing men, with the last
        resounding chord of marble's own leap into song,

would come crashing down, a band of Cossacks stamping
        out an affirmation of the loud and wild reverberations
                of utter human presence, aspiration, act.

Such a buckling of muscle, breath, and lust to prove
        that we exist and that in all creation only we can
                choose to be, to nullify our basic chemistry, become

the incarnate reproductions of our tongues'
        stunning entrechats carved in high relief along
                the wall that separates us from brute silence,

stone and static space and thus, like extinct
        hunters, to survive ourselves as we once did
                in the caves of Altamira — the bright imprints

of our hands (around recumbent bison, leaping
        deer and the retreating boar), fired by the phos-
                phorescence of our kind's longing to endure,

still glowing in the limestone of those walls.
        What if those chiseled replicas, somehow, so be-
                lieved in the figure of the human which they imitate,

in the music pulsing in their veins, you'd swear,
        more absolute than plasma and, suddenly transformed
                by such belief and feeling themselves even only

partly human, they did leap out from this slab
        bolted to the wall? The fission of that cloud
                of marble molecules, still clinging to their backs,

into a mass of sheer amazement in their mouths —
        at the very moment they first sensed the earth's
                vibration at their feet — would disintegrate both

them and us into that pool of excess energy,
        disorder's realm beyond most mortal apprehension,
                except as mathematics for physics' formula and law,

but still forever inaccessible and mute.
        For now, in the afternoon's last slant of light
                receding from that room in Saratoga Springs,

the breath of other poets still buzzing in the glass
        about to shatter, while their tongues' fire echoes
                in the beams and smolders like a brother's threat

of bursting into fierce and all-consuming act
        (remembered one year later here on the coast of Maine
                where the brilliant, blue, relentless music of the sea

sculptures the Atlantic shore with an endless
        tide of aspiration for perfection, mirrored
                by the heaving of the earth, and coastal rocks,

resounding with the moon's galactic pulse,
        are intricately massive incarnations of
                the ever-changing arabesques of waves)

perhaps it is enough to focus what remains
        of attention and desire on that smaller,
                somewhat older figure standing in the distance

of a bas-relief, his trunk almost invisible
        behind the thick and splaying limbs of that
                raucous calabash of singing fellowship.

He is alone, his eyes, his mouth closed and calm,
        his arms gently crossed in total concentration
                on his breast, as if he were utterly fulfilled

with listening, as if no human or inhuman
        sound outside of him could modulate
            the solid vertical of his serenity,

as if he were about to fly back sound-
        lessly into the very origins of sound,
            as if he would efface himself and us in sound.

Red Air

The air above
our village is
bloodred tonight,

as if we lived
on streets with
lava-spewing trees.

But this strange sky
is just the promise
or a threat of snow;

so, we huddle by
our fireplaces,
old woodstoves,

staring at the perish-
able substance
of our flesh and souls.

Tomorrow boys and
girls, come back home
from school, will burn

angelic shadows
on our lawns, then,
frantic to be saved,

raise their ashen
arms and faces toward us
like the immortal

children of Pompeii.

Calco di Cadevere di Donna: *Pompeii*

for John Logan

Lady, I have resurrected this old
    postcard photograph of you while
        rummaging among mementos we accumulate

as proof that we have occupied
    another time and space, perhaps some
        other lifetime, more perfect than this one,

when we were merely tourists in those
    ancient capitals of pain where even
        daily anguish seemed fired to the pitch

of art and we still had faith in beauty
    smoldering at the heart of suffering, needing
        nothing but a glance to flare and suddenly

transform itself from ordinary
    bone, blood and flesh into astounding presence
        and outlast the sound its dying makes.

Lady, I have lived too long and logged
    too many miles on foot to still believe
        this dust that aches my bones and grates my throat

and swirls in fury in my lungs could blaze
    into a beautiful concerto
        and negate the crush of entropy

in every particle of ash of me;
    but your graceful calcified cadaver,
        this cold winter night, rekindles my belief.

That is the perfect posture for anguish:
        your body turned away from it, your face
                buried in your arms, and your enormous

weight balanced on your elbows and your knees;
        with the gentle slope of your long legs,
                the rise and fall of your small hips and breasts

carved by lava's frenzied hand, Lady,
        you're more perfectly human than David
                standing naked in Firenze's public square.

A mother trying to protect
        the petrified fetus inside you,
                you're an ancient lover, too, arched

above the man who's already vanished
        in the very love of you. Solder for an-
                other mouth, your burning lips kiss nothing

but the space beneath them, frozen into
        silence, your smooth buttocks raised above
                your belly, knees and naked feet in anti-

cipation of a pleasure, penetration
        and amazement that may never end —
                that moment of unearthly passion and

anxiety before the barely human
        touches the divine. In one astounding
                instant that the rest of us must struggle

for a lifetime to achieve, you blazed,
        bloomed, and became the consummated gesture,
                word, the emblem that few creatures ever

give to others. In your endless seething,
  endless undulation in the agony
    of passion, that grace which is most ours,

the curved and fragile bridge between
  the terrible and tender, you are
    what this earth, in its decreasing orbit

of the sun, returns to survivors
  and to other lovers sometimes: the name-
    less gift of lava rising from its center

like a tongue reaffirming the sublime
  breath brooding one small egg of glorious
    music in each cell of bone, blood, flesh.

III

Snow has begun to fall, a familiar
  welcomed ash; an alarming fire's
    raging on a distant hill; my wife

and daughter have long faded in the dark-
  ness of my breath; and the veins in both
    my legs throb rivulets of molten rock.

While we remain inhabitants of this
  planet still in flux, through the last
    dimension that will always separate us,

before I fall asleep in nostalgia
  for another place, and with only that
    small space beneath you to be filled

before you walk away, a vision
  consummated without act, tonight, *Donna,*
    I want to slip my body under yours.

Makers and Lovers

to Jocelyn Sloan

As if a speck of diamond dust had lodged
itself under each eyelid
and gently etched the corneas, I close
my eyes and some creature's

crystallized unearthly shape glitters into
focus in the sunlight pooled
beneath my thinning lid, then swims its slow
insistent gallop down

into the darkened caverns of my brain
and just as slowly canters
long and graceful strokes back to the edge
of light. That creature, Jocelyn,

has been roaming in me since my childhood:
it rode the rapids of my blood,
grazed the green herb garden at the center
of my glowing ribs; in dreams

it reared and then leapt from my brow,
a free, ecstatic totem.
Far from the Atlantic coast, its untamed,
more familiar tides, I sit

on a wide, trim sward beside a swimming
pool: rippled by the wind, sun-
light is a cloud of lunar landscapes
sailing at the pit of this

pale green palm of water, always open
like the artificial eye

of a more luxurious race and age
staring blindly at the sun.
Such transformations make me dizzy.

I am a farmer's firstborn
son accustomed to a tougher truth,
a hard-earned, hard-lost vision.
Remembering your love of all that's strong

and beautiful and thrives deep
inside a maker's and a lover's chest,
a hardy cool potato
absorbing minerals from the earth, I close

my eyes to catch that creature's stroking
gallop in the blazing dark
behind my lids again: the hardworking
şea-horse of my name and kind,

bracing moon-hauled tides on his vertical
in a sea of horizontals,
this untamable white beast of beauty's
hunt: the deadly unicorn.

Geese

in memory of Ada and Archibald MacLeish

The scalene angle's point pierces the horizon;
light tears. The V widens for miles. Another.
Then another. The sky darkens, the air throbs
under the pound of wings, cracks to the call
of hundreds of them migrating back to Canada.
After a multithousand-mile flight over oceans
and mountains and jungles and cities, and, almost
home, these geese soar over the last Great Lake,
as sure of their target as missiles or angels
deployed by gods. Unarmed by the awe that fills
our open mouths season after season, all we can
do is stare.
        We are the unbelievers who have
trod the moon's white dust in disbelief and jet-
tisoned magnetic waves of our voice, the radar
of our heart toward uncharted galaxies to trace
even just one other planet's pulse and prove that
in this cosmos we are not unique — only to return
to Earth, the terminus of our trajectory, more
human, more alone.
        Now in the soft tilled loam
of our friend's family garden, as we track today's
last flock of northbound geese, almost invisible
against the darkened sky, we are rooted in a moment
of amazement under arcs of brilliant single sylla-
bles of breath, ignited in our throats and blooming
in the early evening air like exploding rockets
at a local county fair celebrating still another
season's harvest.
        Our faces, our hands are
raised by a supplication that starts in our feet
and clings to the lip of the last wing-feather

as it suddenly bursts into flame with sunlight
and starlight and, a dazzling pentecostal
tongue, plunges deep into the opposite horizon.
Stunned, our arms wrapped around each other in
a warmth of friendship, frost of fear, we walk
back into the house that hovers gently in the dark,
a familiar, ancient ship.

              And when we speak again,
softly, anxious as first lovers or as lovers who
have lived a lifetime when they go to bed, we will
not speak of another season's longing or of one
more and more inexorable migration, but we shall
speak about the garden to be sown, the brilliance
of the stars, this gift that makes our bodies ache.

☒ ☒ ☒ ☒ ☒ ☒ ☒

PART III

☒

Angelic Orders:
A Bestiary of Angels

Fear Survey Schedule

Sirs: In answer to your question-
naire, these are the things
and experiences that cause me
fear or other unpleasant feelings,
and the degree to which by every
one of them I am disturbed.

I am afraid of vacuum
cleaner noises not at all;
a fair amount of open wounds,
enclosed spaces and loud noises.
I am very much disturbed
by dentists, worms and reliquaries.
I am afraid of failure, falling,
and of being left alone, a lot.

I am afraid of blood: a) human,
b) animal, very much; harmless
garden snakes, looking foolish,
of one person bullying another,
angry people, and of weapons.

Of journeys by: a) train, b) bus,
c) cars, I'm not too much
afraid — nor of strangers
and strange shapes, imaginary
creatures. And of sirens
I am not afraid at all.

Birds and bats and mice and cats
cause me unpleasant feelings,
as do commercials, jingles, prayers.

But I am very much afraid
of dead people, elevators,
of darkness and of lightning.
And, I'm afraid, I am afraid
of nude: b) women, a) men
in very high places, singing.

Angelic Orders

I've been seeing angels recently.
Green ones, mostly.
They look like trees.

Some are domestic: fruit trees,
maples, elms, and oaks. They run
after me. They whine when I ignore
them and walk by. They pelt me
with acorns, spit syrup at my head.
They throw tantrums and break birds.

Some are olive trees rooted
for centuries in the stony
landscape of my memory's holy land.
Others are ethereal:
willows rising by the river,
shimmering with ecstasy.

I don't know what to make of one
of them. It's in my bedroom
every night. A cypress, it's
dark green, almost black.

It is tall, serene. Or it trembles,
gathering a storm above a field of red
and fierce, intolerable poppies.
It is glowing softly, moaning.
It is waiting   waiting

Clocks are angels, too:
their phosphorescent faces
glowing pale green through
the night, clucking minutes
one by one and filling up
my room with incandescent
feathers. And radiators,
as I've said before, are
angels. The refrigerator
is an angel: squat and square,
guarding meats and vegetables
and milk inside the steady
cold of its folded wings
where a light mysteriously burns.

The rocking chair's an Early
American Angel. Sometimes,
in the middle of the night,
I wake up and hear it
creaking softly, creaking
like the wrath of God or
the noise among dry bones
waxing louder and louder.

Flags are captured angels.
Flags are captured archangels
tearing their wing tips
on the wind and clawing
for escape. And blankets,
sent from such heights as
lovers come from, are angels.
Asleep, I am thin and white, stirring.

But doors are solid, flat
angels. They are always

there, pure as triangles,
faceless and essential,
locking me out of rivers,
barring me from fields,
from houses, and from mansions
I must enter   I must enter

III

But that is only half
of it. The fact is,
I don't only see

angels, I am one.
When I'm alone
at night, I draw all

the drapes, and in
that total darkness
I become an angel.

I stand stark still
and naked. I don't
stir until I feel

a fierce, unearthly
stirring in the pool
of my belly, the seed

of a thousand saviors
gathering like
a galaxy. My bones

are flutes for the word
of God, and sunlight
streams in my arteries.

At last I glow —
all white. I tremble.
My hair is the moon.

Wingless, unfeathered,
I am translucent.
I am fleshless. Pure.

I rise. I hover
above the city.
I visit virgins.

The Angels of the American Dream

Dazzling and tremendous how quick the sun-rise would kill me,
If I could not now and always send sun-rise out of me.

WALT WHITMAN

We are infested with light.
It gathers on the floor of the sea
that tides in the cave of our pelvis;
it sprouts on the limbs of our lungs,
branches over cliffs in our brain,
a bush burning law in a nation.

An organism from an alien world
rocketed down to test and possess
this planet, it feeds on the darkness
that breeds in the core of our cells,
on the pure filtered air in our blood.
Overnight millions of filaments

root and are thriving. By morning
our skin is transparent, our bones
are black, and we're radioactive,
barbarously bright. Ablaze
with amazement, we stay in our
bed all day, eclipsing the sun

in its orbit. Afraid we'll diffuse,
we don't move, not a muscle
or bone or an eye-beam. Still
by noon we can feel citizens
disintegrating on streets,
murdered by light. Seasons

accelerate. In the wink of an eye,
blossoms are apples that ripen
flames, and clusters of grapes

are coals. Buffalos burn to a crisp
on the spit of their bones. The sea pulls

to a dead stop. Whales rise like zeppelins.
By midnight the earth is pure mineral
ore, melting to white at its center.
Ravenous, we embark

The Angels of Birth

The sun explodes around my house,
blinding as the resurrection.
It is morning. Angels are swooping
purple shadows, shedding their clothes.
Oh, hundreds of naked angels in the naked
air! And Jesus is walking into the east,
the shape of an inviolate man on his back.

From the bedroom, down the stairs,
to the back porch, I stalk a trail
of blood: hands blooming on the walls,
fingerprints frying on the windowpanes.
These aren't my hands, my feet. I will
never find my way out of this labyrinth.

Angels have started attacking my walls,
battering my doors, clawing my windows.
And my name is falling from their mouths,
a skin for the stranger rising in my body.

The Angels of Criticism

They live
in ruins. Each
finger is a different
tool: a little hammer, chisel,
pick. Their thumbs are spades, eyes
the bristles of their souls. Their heads
sluice the darkest past for tiny skulls, for
relics, artifacts of any dried-up god, and their
chests are the empty chambers they pillage. They decipher
the hearts of pebbles. They carve that secret on their wrists
and then they annihilate anyone who will not worship it or needs to.

The Angel of DNA

after a photograph of Joe Brainard by Gerard Malanga

There is nothing behind you but the hint of energy's first spectrum: white to diaphanous gray. Your skull's a prism, the spectral angle jutting out your ear. And the last flagellum's swimming out of sight.

So much of you is missing: your feet tangled in algae, the rippled bark of your calves and thighs, the immeasurable weight and ache of history ripening in your scrotum for the press, the gates of your hips soldered into the fate of male, even your torso, a riverbed without a trace of that one knot to betray your link with others of your kind, the chain that never can be broken. A fugitive from the improbable landscape memory obliterates, you are planted in this plot of time, trapped inside this frame of film like all of us, even if so much of you is missing.

You're the contradiction in our genes we would siphon out, but more elusive than deoxyribonucleic acid. In a glance you're the brink between the brute devouring the marrow to survive and the impossible fusion from father to lover, the pause between the grunt of stones and speech transfigured into song. Your mouth and eyes are the shift from senseless terror to the inscrutable smile of symphonies sculptured by saints. Your hair would turn us into shade, your eyes' brilliant holes of light dissolve us into stones. Afraid to look at you, we can't risk not to: our acid's essential contradiction.

And there is nothing between us, just your fingers curved into the first gesture of a tongue about to curl into a fist by instinct, shatter both of us out of this dimension. Still, I know you, stranger: my lost self betrayed by the mirrors of my eyes, eyelids of my words. I feel you writhing in the thinning space beneath my skin, contradicting who I am and what I do, hauling me beyond the memory of my own measured history, up the sands of a torrential river, back into a blinding spectrum.

Until then, except for our hands and tongues arched toward one another and the rays of our eyes refracted by the lens our breath's about to cloud, there is nothing between us.

The Angels of Eternal Life

If they remain alone, they never die.
Their unmatched molecules are perfect,
charged with energy distilled of
entropy. Forever radiant with that
one moment when they were utterly
happy and fulfilled light-years before
their birth, their eyes are moons
staring at the sun, all day, all night.

But they have to know each other. So
they walk the streets, searching empty
eyes of other beautiful strangers,
desperate for one glimpse of such in-
human ecstasy. And when they find
each other, look, then stare with all
the fury of their awesome loneliness,
slowly they become transfigured into
lovers married years ago, fading and
defaced reflections of each other.

The Angels of Film

Eyes. Eyes. They are the eyes
that feed on children in the sun,
on brides, birds, grandmothers, stars.
They're always there, loaded revolvers
blinking too loudly at parties, shooting
at smiling faces with more vengeance
than crime or conscience. They capture
our gestures, helpless in their sight,
just to prove the past or present real.
We were children, once; beneath this
face there is another we have never
wanted. Our bodies just keep going,
developing reproductions of ourselves.
Our souls are prisoners of eyes forever.

The Angel of the Gate

after a photograph of David Ignatow by Gerard Malanga

The gate is closed and guarded: veiled figures kneeling in their vigil, a kaddish of rock salt. A cross with broken arms leans like that obelisk near you cracking at the base. Lapped blank by rain, the sun's rough eager tongue, a slab slants to mark and close the angle's mouth. But yards of ground shrink back, sink to nourish the famished dead under the gentle weight of your eyes desperate to forgive and rescue them and us.

You aren't the center of this scene. You've been here all your life, one foot rooted in the ivy rooted in the eyes and throats, the pelvis of our common family. Off to one side and alone, your voice's bitter wisdom still charts avenues and roads, spans the gulf between worlds. Your words are clay bricks, markers for the murders of our love, monuments of what we are and do and leave behind.

If you turned to look this way right now, the earth would open like a broken eye, and the grass, the trees, our headstones, and our history would slip back into the gullet of that first and final film.

Instead, turn your back on us. Walk toward the world you've glimpsed behind the world. Release the giant in the dwarf. Let the leper bloom. Call the shrapnel of the factory worker back into a human shape. Charge the electric chair with grace. Give us the indestructible pulse of our own hearts again.

We'll follow. Speak: the gate will fly open.

The Angel of the Henhouse

You were bigger than me.
Your front teeth were separated
and you could whistle through them.
In the summer, when we drank
from the faucet near the barn,
you could squirt water
through your teeth, one long
stream, clear as a whistle.
You were Uncle Larry's pet.

You were stronger than me.
You could carry two baskets
full of eggs, one in each hand,
carry them downstairs even
on ice-covered steps in winter.
I slipped once, and the eggs,
a hundred melting suns,
crackled on the crusted ice.

You were older than me.
One day while Uncle Larry slept,
a self-made messenger from god
under a tree, you took me, your
captured cowboy, to your henhouse
tent where dust was piled high
as sunlight, and like a savage man

of medicine, with a feather's blade,
you opened up a wound in me to rid
my body of that arrowhead. Then
you taught me how to leave the echo
of your inhuman camouflage behind,
the figure of an angel in the dust.

The Angel of Imagination

I've been writing poems all night long.
Oh the lies and lovers I've invented,
the beautiful beasts I've become, more
awesome than those ageless archangels
in planetary jungles. And all night, in
the back corner of my eye, a face has
been staring at me, an enormous eye.

It has drilled a hole into my skull and
sees me through and through. It knows
the truth at the heart of lies, the lies
that are the strata of all art, and,
offering me a glimpse of the only world
I ever want to see, all night the echo
of a voice that is the spit and image
of my own has begged: *Dive into my iris.*

The Angels of the Jungle

The traffic of tourists has stopped.
The workers' trucks are still
silent. Above the humming of this
night's red heart, voices from lost
jungles are asking the same questions
over and over again: *Adam, where are*
you? Where is your brother, Abel?
Tonight I won't be the one to answer.

The Angels of Knowledge

Once they drank an indecipherable language
from a spring of wisdom at the center of
the jungle. They spoke with stars and were
murdered for what their tongues could never
translate into human thought or conquest,
greed, the power to rule space and atoms.

Generations of a forest rooted in this
earth's trembling core, their hearts
pumped a sap that was green with mystery.
Now each tiny leaf tongues its revenge:
no one can hear them and survive. You
fall into fits of knowledge, shuddering
a deadly wisdom. Mastered, your souls
fertilize their roots, their highest branch.

The Angels of Love

Disguised as shapes you love, lovers, friends,
and spouses, they are the princes of beasts.
You never learn to fear them or wage war
against them till they're just about to kill you.
Instead, you believe you are the creature
that they say you are. When your friend says
your right hand hurts him, cut it off.
Tear out your tongue: it can never please
your lover. Give your children your eyes.
Here, love, eat the heart of my last hope.

The Angel of Molecules

All day I've refused to be
everything I am: husband,
father, friend, and enemy
of any other living thing.
My will agreed and vanished
into space. But the slag
of cells, of history, my own
three decades of illusions
simply wouldn't melt. Then
tonight I began to feel all
my atoms rarefy. There!
I was that window... chair
... menorah... knife...
O angel of molecules, quick,
before I become this wor....

The Angels of New England

The rat's angelic chatter in the attic
and the furnace moaning its white fire
are familiar winter choruses in this
New Hampshire house shedding a century
of paint. And when the wind has died,
and if we hold our breath, from
the forest's heart of ice we can hear
the soft sweet vowels of our witches
singing as they burn.
                              Tonight the dark is
heavy on our lips, a yard of ground frozen
solid to its burning core. The white breath
of snow sprouts between the rocks; and chairs,
angel-headed tombstones glowing pale
as ice in moonlight, crouch. Under our
inherited handcarved headboard, waiting
for the slow loosening of our muscles'
rigor, we lie still as still-warm corpses
waiting for another song, a warmth, a sleep.

The Angel of Oblivion

The sun sucks mist out of your glass
skin. You shimmer, purer than dis-
tilled water. You're so luminous,
your ice-bones crack in calm frenzy.

O angel of oblivion, obliterate me
more. Wipe out my eyes. Spin my
spine with outrageous intent. Throw
me down in a fit of tongues I will
never remember. Burn another hand
full of cells. Make my future past.

The Angels of Poetry

Encapsulated in a ball of glass,
in that vacuum they are nothing,
invisible to the naked human eye.
Still, they think they are all those
images they feed on and believe
their voices magnify them into gods
prophets speak of, stones adore.

But no one's ever heard a thing
they've said. One was seen once:
a tiny thing, its head a speck
of mirror flashing a flea's tooth.
Still, they believe and sing at
such an inhuman pitch only dogs
and porpoises can hear, and
everything around them vanishes.

The Angels of Quasars

They're coming. Every night
I hear them coming: the whine
of their ships' incredible

annunciations far above
the cornfields at the city's
edge in the enormous dark

among the stars. Only dogs
and others like me hear them.
Their fantastic engines ring

grace in our bones. One day
they won't simply hover over
fields, visions for a few in-

somniacs. But they'll land.
They'll land swiftly, without
warning, right in the centers

of cities. As if promised
for centuries, they will dis-
embark, radiant, inhuman, and

glorious as gods stalking virgins.

The Angels of Radiators

Every night when my wife
and daughter are asleep
and I'm alone in this old house
lost in landscapes somewhere
between the points of stars,
my furnace fails like heaven.

The water that will turn
to steam and turn to heat
and rise as grace runs out.
In unlighted corners, angles
opening to blank space,
radiators, cold and white,
are silent and dead angels,
incarnate where they fell.

Every night, every winter,
I have to go down cellar,
turn the valve until the gauge
is full of water once again,
until the furnace starts
to rumble with its resurrection.
Then the house begins to move,
and through the winter night
that threatens us like Hell, by God,
the pure spirit of the fire roars
blue, veins ring, and radiators,
a whole chorus of Dominions, sing
and dance wild alleluias warm as spring.

The Angels of the Suburbs

Their faces are five fragile petals, delicate
unearthly velvet stitched by a single thought,
their very source and center. They're so thin,
they disappear in sunlight, evaporate in wind.
They stare at everyone with the serene surprise
the slaughter of sons couldn't alter. If you
stare back, you'll never be happy again or want
to. Their thought is relentless and implacable,
until they're blinded by night.
                          Only then, if
you listen, if you listen with a mystic's ear
lost in ecstasy, or as someone intent on learning
all the secrets of the earth, you might feel
their invisible fragrance singing by a window,
rising from the feet of cliffs, or falling off
rooftops. When you do, anchor yourself. Burn
blessed candles in both ears. Cut off your legs.

The Angels of Transmigration

They come in the middle of the night, in the dark.
Their bodies lost in shadows, their fur glows
with veins of gold and silver buried in them.
They speak to me with the sweet voices of lovers,
promising to tell me all the secrets of the dead,
show me the cities of ancient gods, future races,
and leave their precious antlers as gifts. But
they refuse to say what they'll ask for in return:
light, love, the mystery of children and of breath.

I won't comply. Bone and metal slash my sides.
My room trembles with the ecstatic cry of martyrs,
soldiers, my father's voice eaten by cancer's mechanisms.
This is the language of drills, the vowels of guns,
a tongue the dead teach to the living for the future.
Then in the morning's first, most fragile light,
brass hooves pound my chest; the smell of tombs
lost for centuries in the desert and the fine
metallic dust of holy hunters gather in my mouth.

The Angels of the Underground

As if called by a voice
inhabiting the sun
crouching on a hilltop
and brooding over suburbs,
they come from behind
the gray, loose bark of
trees, beneath a stone.
They rise from the bone
and flesh of cattle
steaming in the fields
and alleys. They come
from the folds and seams
of our damp clothes, from
the roots of our hair.
They come from nowhere.

This morning the space
outside our window
filled with a universe
of seeds. Tonight swarms
of newborn larvae
gather into trembling
blue-green nebulae
inheriting our air.

And worms are stirring
under our soles,
rising to be crowned
princes of the earth.

The Angels of Vietnam

The morning liquefies.
I take one step, spring
up, and I am swimming
above branches of coral.
I breathe water. Delicate
fish dart through my eyes.
Gold and black, they are
angels nesting in my lungs.
And inside my skull they
sing shrill, barbarous
arias, chorales of kyries
at some inhuman pitch.
They shatter my bones.

Nothing weighs me down.
Men flicker like matches.
Whole cities are burning.
The Mississippi shines
with blood. I am rising
higher and higher. Whales
are winging me toward
planets pulsing like pearls,
space infested with sharks.

The Angel of the Wolf Pack

Animals stumble in pairs toward a tideless sea.
Blood floods the womb of all she-creatures.
Even the tiniest fetus stirring is aborted.

The angel's at my door, mouth frothing with moon.
His breath is warm against the transparent glass
of my skin. His paws stroke my hips and flanks.
His snarl unlocks a savage memory inside my cells.

I cling to the wilderness of his mane.
I give myself to him.
An emptiness in me I'd never known begins to fill
with his sweet foam. I will bear us a new breed.

The Angels of Xanadu

Springing from the dark
cool caverns in the earth,
fountains rising from
their own reflections,
willows on the muddy river-
bank are wholly still,
the palest green, waiting
to erupt, spit the lava
of their sap, shudder
glowing cinders, showers
that will singe our lips
with mystery and gentleness,
and solder them with grace
we will never understand.

The Angels of Youth

Wingless, the babies scratch
in the corner shadows, their skin
shredded into fur. They snap
at your ankles, their eyes fierce
as knotholes in the sunlight
burning the walls of old barns.
If you look into them, you can see
the horror of your most private
hope. You climb the attic stairs.

Filling the sudden explosion of
dark, the shapeless memory of un-
remembered guilt, a terrible angel.
He raises one calm wing up to a beam,
and with the other gently offers you the rope.

The Angel of Zealots

I can hear you pacing
up and down between
our beds every night.

Your soles are silent,
as if, every night, you,
like a mystic, suffer

levitation for our sakes
and souls, and, chaste,
your body is as light

as dust, as silent
as the dark you are.
Only your rosary clicks.

You finger your beads:
dried bones of fetuses
answer your prayers.

In this third-story
hall hung with dead
Christs, three times

removed from both
the city and the world
below, we lie in rows,

sleepless as saints.
A bloodless bat,
you are our guardian

angel rustling nearby,
Gabriel at the door
of Eden, sword in hand,

driving us back in
until we have no choice
but to reinvent our sin.

Lucifer, Falling

My right calf has ached all week.
I was afraid of varicose veins
and blood clots. Now the ache's
reached the tendons just above
my ankle. God! I can feel my
right foot hardening into horn.

PART IV

Letters from the Tower

Letters from the Tower

(Yaddo)

I

Every morning for the last two weeks, with nothing
    but blank sheets of paper and some sharpened pencils
        — tools of the only trade I know — I've climbed

the narrow tower stairs into this high-ceilinged
    cell with its walls painted a pale ivory, sparsely
        furnished with a logic not my own: a chaise longue

and a cot, a *prie-dieu* leaning toward the bust
    of a sinister and adolescent saint near a picture-
        window overlooking distant mountains stretching out

beyond a vast expanse of swards sloping toward
    formal gardens of rare roses where granite statues
        of imported Grecian women, hoisting urns of what

must be ointments of crushed petals and exotic
    spices on their shoulders, keep a mute, immobile
        vigil near the flashing splash of man-made waterfalls.

Gazing down on such preternatural splendor,
    I could be a banished prince, the true successor
        to the throne, condemned here by my bastard brother,

His Majesty the King, to contemplate my fate,
    renounce all worldly goods, the glories of the soil,
        prepare my common soul for its imminent decapitation.

In this excess of white hush, I might be an abbess
    come to meditate on Mary's sorrowful mysteries,
        my old and heavy body hovering about the room

in an anticipation of a modified assumption…. Shit,
    what's a peasant farmer's son doing here in this
        anachronistic fantasy of a decadent Victorian

who soothed her nerves, assuaged her pain by soaking
    her left hand in a basin full of warm opals while
        her *Della Robbian* dentist filled her mouth with gold?

I haven't come here every day to participate
    in anybody's history but my own. My memory
        is my only prison, premise, and assumption,

towering above the rubble of a life I worked
    and plotted to erect, then willfully demolished.
        My friend, like you I've come here to survive myself.

                Forgive me for not having heard
                what your silence was saying more clearly;
                I was busy calling you deaf.

                II

                I dream I can no longer

                tell the screams of a human from those of a jay:
                streetcurses, brakesqueal, sirens,
                the whining of a child, the sobs of a hostile lover,
                dreams of real wilderness, all muffled. . .

But Christ, who *can* survive in such rarefied sur-
    rounds? The brilliant jams and marmalades shimmering
        in silver bowls beside the ringing crystal Waterfords;

morning eggs floating in a halo of fresh butter
    gleaming on the Limoges china as translucent
        as the wrists of wealthy dowagers in sunlight;

the literary pleasantries of the languid
    cocktail hour; the intimate exchange of gossip
        and of intimate neuroses; the orchestrated dinner

bells; the recitals in the private chapel
    after dinner; applause polite as murmured litanies;
        the whisper of long skirts across the parquet floors;

the slow, restrained, soft clicks of brass latches, locks and bolts.
    After all this luxury of manifest civility,
        when we are left with nothing but relentless

echoes in our chests, the utter destitution
    in our souls, the brutal silence of a night
        that may not end, of a morning that will surely

dawn too soon, my friend, will we comrades in art
    also spend this night contemplating the revolver's open
        mouth, the mantra pulsing from a stolen carving knife,

the lilting hum of phenobarbital and gin?
    And when dawn breaks, at last, will we awaken
        to discover that tableau and frieze — the massacre

of lovers, spouses, children that we planned
    and executed — intricately etched
        on the insides of our corneas?

I dream I am a siren singing underwater,

having lured myself to death.

III

What we deny, denies us.
What we make live in art denies us

if the blood spilled to it is anyone's
but our own. All else is white sound. . .

With my lunch pail in one hand, papers in
       the other, I climb those stairs again, a faithful
             factory hand off to another day of honest work.

I could become accustomed to this way
       of life. While sunlight settles in the paint,
             I review the products of my last two shifts:

White sound.
       Calculated to drown out the more
             human noises of the heart, the howling

of the beast that crouches in the darkness
       of the brain. In self-disgust I turn to
             the work of a revolutionary city woman.

                   How dare we call the scream of a jay
                   its natural sound simply because

White sound.
       The static of half-truths that would erase
             the cries of more than half the human race

             we've never heard it sing?

and in the black light of day come crashing
       down in its maker's complicated heart
             under the weight of history, day-to-day

                   Things happen
in translation.

reality, a chorus of mythology.
    Listen, I'm a mill hand's and a farmer's
        son. I know the smell of blood spilled by

my own hand, in this life and that other.
    The whine of a hundred looms all in one
        room, the grunting howl of pigs that are being

led to slaughter, the grunt men make
    as they break, alone or with an other —
        all echo in my tonsured head, in each

cell of this body I have worked so hard
    to make delicate, refined, to generate its own
        white sound.

The death toll

mounts in Florida, where I was born —
black bodies falling like needles

Listen, who said these cultivated flower
    gardens, these rustic neoclassic paths
        among the pines, these forsythias

from a white pine tree. A volcano erupts.
Nothing so pacified, inert, or tame

masquerading as the burning bush
    on Sinai aren't the jungle they have
        always been? Who said the death toll would be

it can be trusted beyond a certain solstice
of gratuitous pain; the well-meant joke
of sex or race

higher in a southern city than in
　　these northern hills? Who believes the blood
　　　　of Cain flows less in the veins of artists

　　　　　　the teller can afford to not hear clearly,
　　　　　　all honorable men counting on laughter

than in our common laborers', regardless
　　of our color, sex? And when Sappho chiseled
　　　　her commandment forbidding mourning in

　　　　　　to drown out the rude Polack strains
　　　　　　of a Chopin etude. If a woman paces

a home of poetry, who said that in
　　her other hand she wasn't holding
　　　　the bloody disembodied head of Orpheus?

　　　　　　in her room, black fists clenched white
　　　　　　with anger; if a woman works in her cabin

White sound.
　　Every woman's death diminishes you
　　　　and me more, every man's. And still, and still,

　　　　　　defying terror to understand another
　　　　　　woman on her page; if a woman stalks

we and our art live by the death of others;
　　and the blood that's spilled to it, the blood
　　　　that steams in slaughterhouses, battlefields,

　　　　　　herself on canvas; if a woman
　　　　　　builds herself a jade burial armor;

in the endless privacy of bathtubs is
        anybody's but our own. Listen,
                the crow and cardinal caw and sing

                        if a woman walks in the woods and walks
                        and walks and grinds her white forehead

to one another. The wild rabbit devours
        the forsythia. Your pet cat offers you
                the mangled, almost bloodless corpse

                        against indifferent moss and weeps
                        and rages at such weeping, what does it mean?

of the robin that's been hatching her blue
        eggs outside my study window —
                a humble homage to the hand that

                        If a woman falls in the forest and
                        no one hears, is there sound?

feeds her in the house of poetry where
        she was abandoned by another poet.
                Next door, a woman and a man are making

                        If a man falls in the forest and
                        no one hears…

love. In our respective cells,
        you and I are making poems about
                men and women making love and war.

                                        Things happen
                in translation.

White sound.

IV

There is a poem missing here
like the deliberate flaw the Navajo weaver
leaves in her blanket — to let the soul out.
That poem would be a luxury, a passion;
it could afford trust, it could have something
to do with love...

I've been thinking about men all day, the sound they make when there's
no one around to hear them weaving sounds around a flaw for their
heart's own slow release.

This is the sound the newborn man-child makes as his foreskin is sliced
off for sanitary purposes that will not save his body or his soul.

This is the sound the adolescent boy makes in his dreams as the stranger
with his father's voice laughs at that useless labia wrapped around his
thing, then hacks it off with his hunting knife.

This is the sound that young men make when they sit together drinking,
talking on a porch in Saratoga Springs in a loneliness that will never
be consoled, and suddenly their words stiffen their own tongues like
violent strangers' cocks inside their mouths.

This is the sound men make when the silence at the sight of a sudden
tenderness in them shrivels up their eyes like testicles unexpectedly
immersed in the cold blue of the Atlantic.

This is the sound men make when the seeds of some unspeakable love in
them die in the pit of their own hands and suddenly burst into flames
like sons.

This is the sound men make as they fall into pools of sunlight on the for-
est floor beneath the weight and worry of the unsung music in the
story of Ulysses and Penelope.

This is the sound of one old man, drunk on brandy, as he tapdances his Step-'n-Fetch routine alone in the moonlight when there's no one near to comfort him at dawn.

This is the sound men make as they vanish in the canvas that they thought they'd filled with their own lives.

This is the sound of men shattering in an intolerable symphony of muscle.

This is the sound men make when, because of mindless pleasantries of sex or race, their white fists pound brick walls until they're blue, then black, then bloody as a buck nigger's on the rack.

This is the sound of young men in a hundred foreign fields as they collapse beneath the kiss of their stranger brothers' bullets.

This is the sound of men in cubicles and cells, in jails, monasteries, submarines, as they invent themselves, trace the contours of their bodies with a creator's care, fill each other with the tender hum and power of their very lives, then, like ancient women, lie there as their souls escape through the flaws of their own hearts — with passion, trust, perhaps something to do with love.

This is the sound a boy makes as he's raped by his mother's or his father's lover.

This is the sound men make in their terrifying love of daughters who can never be protected from the sound men make.

This is the sound men make in the threadless maze of their love of women and of one another.

This is the sound of one man, forever in a forest of white sound, falling.

⊠ ⊠ ⊠ ⊠ ⊠ ⊠ ⊠

PART V

⊠

A Nest of Sonnets

These harbingers of spring are really dumb.
Winter isn't over yet; the trees
aren't in full bloom; the weatherman still sees
a chance of frost; the worms are all quite numb
with their long sleep deep in the thawing ground.
But here is robin redbreast, hard at work
on this year's nest; the tomcat goes berserk;
a thin snow starts to fall without a sound.

These birds will risk their lives just to insist
on summer, sing until our bones turn green
and blossom into song, until our lean
but swelling tongues cry out: "Robin, desist!

Your wiser brothers send you on ahead
to find out whether we're alive or dead."

Now why does that forsythia insist
on masquerading as the burning bush?
Such beauty ought to know how to resist
that old temptation, know how not to rush

right in where even Moses never trod.
No wonder birds don't nest inside its limbs.
Their lives are tough enough; they've learned to dread
the law asserting beauty skims

the terror from the truth. The hares begin
to nibble at the fiery blooms. Too soon
the burning petals of that bush, at noon,
will fizzle, fall, the core of beauty's sin:

to worship galaxies of burnt-out stars
that never saved us from our lust and wars.

A woodsy drama is unfolding here:
the robin's hatching this year's brood; she flits
from hemlock to the lawn, where she just sits
and stares back at the sun till she can hear
a worm start stirring underfoot.

                              Nearby,
the chipmunk's silly with the smell of eggs;
he sniffs and skitters on his tiny legs
as if waltzing on blue shells.
                              The grackle, high
atop the pine, sits patiently and mute.
And while the robin makes the chipmunk scoot,
attacks him like a hawk or simply begs
him off, the grackle gobbles up the eggs.

Ah, redbreast, if your enemy can't kill
your babies, then your sister surely will.

      ✠   ✠   ✠

The sound of copulation's in the air!
A bright red cardinal repeats his mate's
own blazing passion; and the robin baits
the robin with her warble. Here and there

the bees begin to pollinate the air,
their breathless hum the buzz of sperm, while doves
coo-coo the wiser notes of their long love's
refrain and young boys whistle everywhere

they go to chase the girls. We must beware
of so much propagation, so much song
in spring, remember winter nights are long
and poems fruitless to the heart that's bare.

Ah, Love, why hunt for rhymes, when everywhere
the sound of copulation's in the air!

❊   ❊   ❊

I'm getting sick of all this tender rustic stuff
about the birds and bees, the robin on the wing.
It's autumn in my life; I know it isn't spring.
I think the time has come for someone to get rough.

A farmer's son, I haven't worked hard all my life
escaping from the farm in me, to come full cir-
cle back to plowing trusty mother nature. Sir,
there must be more to art and life than simply *life*.

I want to murder and create (perhaps a hit
on Broadway) characters on a much grander scale,
then live like royalty just off the sale.
I want to write an epic celebrating *shit*.

For stronger muses there is always tougher meat
than birds and bees and sonnets plodding on six feet.

The weatherman was right, of course: last night
a frost that threatened the forsythia,
our new tomato plants, and made plasma
in our tongues freeze at the pitch of fright,

our conversations elegies of loss.
It will take days to know what did survive,
what perished. Lord, up here we seem to thrive
because the loaded odds sift out the dross,

the timid and too frail. We can depend
on summer being just as long and fierce,
on sunlight that's so bitter it can pierce
you to the bone. Who knows how it will end.

The battle isn't over yet, redbreast:
the kiss of frost still lingers on your nest.

But look, while we were worrying to death
about our flowers' fate, our lettuce patch,
this bird did what she'd meant to do: just hatch
her eggs. Her babies throb with their first breath,

each heartbeat more astounding than the first.
And yet, though three chicks more than fill the nest,
there were four eggs. What tiny fetal test
condemned the fourth, what urgent bloody thirst

that could be satisfied with one blue egg?
But why should greater logic rule *their* lives?
In any sphere, what will survive, survives:
an armless man, a chicken with one leg.

These chicks can't fret their temporary plight,
when all their instincts concentrate on flight.

These moths won't settle for a simple death
like birds. They have to be theatrical,
like poets restless for ethereal
rewards so much they simply hold their breath.

So that one drowns in your last glass of scotch
or kamikazes your lit cigarettes;
another loiters as if taking bets
his fizzle will be brighter, he won't botch

his final exit. This one's wings are spread
into a white and delicate tutu;
then, when her beauty's captivated you,
she spins atop her head until she's dead.

I won't be conned by flashy suicide;
my dance with death will be one long, slow stride.

Well, Wildebeest, what do you think of that?
You stare at me as if you knew just one
small useless fact that might restore the fun
I lost to art. You silly household cat,

about this business you know less than I
do. You get your three meals a day on time
and you sleep mindlessly until the chime
awakens you in time to watch the sky

for birds that fly as soundless as a dream,
as bloodless. Just what did you do today
to earn your name as predator and prey,
to prove you aren't the neutered pet you seem?

Your speechless answer tumbles from your mouth:
another songbird that will not fly south.

Coda

Where is the sleeping farmer's son in me
who reaps these sonnets of anxiety?

�   ✜   ✛

Biddeford Pool

for Alan Mariani

Whoever you are, to you endless announcements!
WALT WHITMAN

This fish-shaped village
of some ten or twenty
fishermen might be another
Paumanok for some other poet.

Standing in the marshes
near the ancient wharves
still smelling of the sea,
some queer split-tongued
bird of mysterious genesis,
he could stretch his neck
and sing large and rugged songs,
endless announcements of immor-
tality to the village fishermen.

But I've seen the way
these eight-fingered men look
at seagulls and at cranes
when they return from mornings
spent on the horizon's edge.

Their eyes are blind with sun-
light. Their tongues are split
with salt, their mouths white
with brine, as if they'd bitten
into death. Grunting and
lamenting, they haul in their nets
to repair them and their history.
And I know what they would do
to anyone who stood around
and sang and sang and sang.

The Slaughter of Pigs

to Daphne

We take our goblets of red dinner wine
into the living room, light
glass candles whose pale glow's scented with
the fragrance of fresh pine, and

we stretch out on the white wool rug, as if it
were an island beach that shelved
on some other time and place. From the heart
of arctic wastes that once shaped

this landscape we inhabit, a storm is
raging in another year.
We watch snowflakes disappear into
the gullet of a howling

wind, and I remind you of the time we
stood by another window
in another storm. Pointing to the flakes,
you softly sang: "Oh, Daddy, see,

they look like fishes diving into the ground!"
Daphne, tonight you're far more
fragile than you were years ago when
I first held you in my arms

ten minutes after birth, before you'd had
the time to be transformed from
some primal creature (the milky lunar
casing of the womb still clinging

to your flesh) into my daughter, into this
young woman who, with those wiles

you're just discovering you have, convinces
me to slaughter your pink pig.

Our living room becomes a barnyard; we
lay the pig down on its back;
you squeal as if you were a baby once
again; you offer me the knife.

❉   ❉   ❉

I slip the carving knife into your pig's
tough underside, guide the blade
up to its bloodless, silent throat as if
I had done this all my life…

and that high breathless wheeze, that childish
whine of frantic pigs rises
once again above clean pails of steaming
blood in Dingley's slaughterhouse.

Sledgehammers thud another snout; and when
its skin and bristles have been
tenderized in vats of boiling water,
its carcass pulleyed up, when

it hangs there in fall light, its hooves
dancing softly on the wooden floor,
its head thrown back in sheer abandonment
to hide some soundless promise

of revenge raging in its small blind eyes —
like the bloated body of
a pink and hairy criminal left on
the scaffold as an omen —

with the calm precision of a surgeon,
Dingley slits the pig's soft breast
and belly and leaps back, just as the rush
of viscera and bowels

fills a washtub, their sweet odor fills our
lungs, and vomit fills my mouth
again and then again. We load the tub,
the pails of blood, the carcass

on our pickup truck. Dingley wipes his brow,
waves a bloody hand and grins.
As we haul our load away, we hear sledge-
hammers thud another snout.

       ❎   ❎   ❎

Like a witness's at an execution,
your eyes flash wide with horror,
then with tender fascination. But I tell
you, Daphne, there's no pleasure

and no pity in this childhood story.
Such slaughter's just another
way of life. Hitler had invaded France;
our uncles wrote us from somewhere

in the Orient; Kamikaze dove
into our dreams; and Roosevelt
inspired us to greater and still greater
sacrifice, until every

simple human thing we did became
a total act of war and
this world a planetary charnel house.
We hoarded cans, glass, rubber bands

to be melted down and molded into
deadly weapons; blue-flowered
sacks of chicken-feed became my sister's
dresses and then rags to wash

the windows, floors; once a day we gathered
eggs; once a week, with an ax
in one hand and a squawking chicken in
another, my father walked

up to the tree stump out behind the barn
and in a simple, graceful
act, seemingly enlisting every
muscle in his body, he

chopped off the chicken's head,
tossed the torso down, and waited
patiently while that decapitated
hen waltzed around him spinning

bright trapezoids of blood, until she
toppled long enough for him
to chop her legs off; and we played with them,
tugged the tendons that made those

scaly claws work: close, open, close, while Father
hunted through the entrails for
a soft-shelled egg, a gizzard and a liver.
At suppertime we listened

to the news on our kitchen radio, wrote
letters and wrapped packages
of chocolate bars and chewing gum for our
uncles, for our neighbor's son.

We wasted nothing. If we couldn't use
or eat or barter whatever

came into our lives, we shipped it to
the front to save another

life or waste it for our own life's sake.
And for our winter's table
far from battlegrounds, for our survival
and his own, Father slaughtered pigs.

⌗   ⌗   ⌗

But how we pampered them to death! For months we hunted new toma-
toes burnt by an unexpected frost or too much sun, sweet ears of corn
attacked by worms, and eggs too blood-speckled to be sold or used.
                                                            We
saved stove and table scraps, from seeds to onion skins, leftovers from
the plates of dogs and cats, stale breads and pastries salvaged from the lo-
cal bakery. We stirred them all into barrels of buttermilk, milk we couldn't
sell, milk we could do without.
                    Sometimes it seemed that food was taken
from our mouths just to fatten pigs for slaughter, as our days unfolded
in a constant calendar of unquestioned rebirth and destruction, each
human, animal and vegetable feeding off the other.
                                        After supper dogs
sniffed out the weasels and raccoons that came to graze in our cabbage
patch at night. Cats hunted rats and field mice, trapping them before
they ate the eggs we'd come to gather in the morning. If one hen was
wounded and we didn't notice her, the other hens pecked at her
wound, satisfying their own thirst for blood.
                                        The cows chomped on
the hay reaped from the fields where we had spread cow manure in the
spring: we drank the sweet and foaming milk, still warm. And in fall we
harvested a winter's store of vegetables from our garden fertilized by
cow dung. What was taken from our mouths to feed the animals and
earth, in time, returned into our mouths as food.

When pigs were slaughtered, the women also had to work even harder. Pigs were essential, long-lasting, worthy of the work. No part of the pig would go to waste if it could be made into some kind of winter fare in a symphony of old recipes that mothers sang as lullabies to their small breast-feeding daughters, near the kitchen stove, in the darkness of the long and lonely cycles of survival among those farming women.

Sometimes the work at slaughter-time killed one of us, while others simply died at war.

⊠　⊠　⊠

Too young for the First, just barely too old
for the Second, my father
never went to war and never taught me
how to hunt. When their fathers

bought them BB guns and my friends shot
pigeons off the grange hall roof,
pretending those dumb birds that ate dry crumbs
out of our hands were Jap planes,

or later, when they went hunting with
their fathers, downed their first doe
or buck, skinned it, nailed the trophy of those
antlers on their fathers' barns

and, with manly pride glowing in their clouding
eyes, relived their hunting trip —
the stalking, silent waiting, every last
detail up to that breathless

moment when they stared deep into the eyes
of deer before pumping just one
slug into the heart of their stunned skulls,
filling those boys with release…

almost as much fun as jerking off when
you're alone at night in bed
or waking up in the middle of a good
wet dream — my father

said I wasn't old enough to play with
guns. He worked in the shipyard
every day, often overtime. And once
I borrowed Harold Dingley's

BB gun. I shot at the grange hall
roof: all the pigeons fluttered
in a slow ascension of annoyance
and flew off toward the henhouse —

then one arced across the sky, across my
eye clouded by the blazing
sun, veered toward that small grove of pines
near the henhouse, just behind

the pigpen, suddenly collapsed as if
under the enormous weight
of its own life, and crashed through the branches
out of sight. When I found it

in a brilliant pool of bloodless sunlight,
its whole body throbbed with each
heartbeat, and the tiny eye at the center
of its head burned more fiercely

than the sun blaring overhead, the song
of cicadas ringing
like the ping of bullets ricocheting
in an amphitheater

of raw steel. For a moment lasting longer
than the memory of war,

I pumped pellet after pellet into
that bird's head, that ferocious sun, until

I caught my breath, until the sun, the eye,
the entire head was gone.
Daphne, my father never taught me how
to hunt. I taught myself to kill.

⊠   ⊠   ⊠

Where is my mother in this story? She
is alone in the kitchen
of our small upstairs apartment in
Grandpa Poulin's house and she

is singing, mending, she is baking; she
is lying on her back; her
muscles cramp and cervix welds and she
can't grunt or scream me out of her;

the fontanels of my own skull in her
refuse to fold and, as her
blood singes the low ceiling of her
bedroom, I'm ripped out of her

with forceps; the doctor drops me on her
bed, insists I'm dead, that she's
the only one to save; Aunt Marie, her
midwife, lifts and plunges me,

still blue and breathless, and baptizes me
in cold common water: *Je
te baptise au nom du Père, et du Fils,
et du Saint-Esprit.* And I

am born in blood and water. She and I
survived each other. Now she
is sewing, mending, baking still, and I
still hear the echo of her

voice sing out my father's name and mine, and I
sing back to her until I
come home for supper after dark, and we
rest, father, mother, me.

        ⊠   ⊠   ⊠

This winter storm is as relentless as
a father's memory. Plows
carve wide palpable circles of caution
around our house. Standing by

the window, I stare at the falling snow
as someone in a speeding
car believes he could be moving toward
the calmer center of a storm...

and I'm standing on the tip of that raft's
high diving board in
the middle of the pond, my whole body
addled by the height and dazzle

of refracted sunlight in the water
far below, a boy's senseless
ecstasy of being, of just being
this small boy with a new pale

dust of hair on my arms and legs, around
my groin that aches at night
for reasons all its own. I take the deepest
breath I can, leap as high as

my will will carry me and, with my calves
stiffened, my feet kneaded to
a blunt point, plunge into the center
of the sun. Water opens,

a warm and total memory. Pliable
as lead, my muscles sink me
down until water thickens to a cool
and ancient slime, until

I'm buried to my waist in stirring
earth where uncreated
species sleep. I hover in that breathless
dream I've dreamed before, until

my ribcage starts to cave in with a wish
for gills, my arms frantic
to be fins. I must surface. My eyes open.
Above me, sunlight ripples,

a green and shimmering breath, so high
I'd open my mouth
for a hook. One more thrust of that small tail
contracting into legs, one

more shove of arms that grow against the odds,
their fingers webbed with water,
one more drop of breath breathed in another
world, trailing clouds of slime,

a molten skin emulsified by sun-
light, gasping for dear life,
my head tears the last membrane of water
into air that takes root

in my lungs again. My thin hair matted
to my skull, my face still blue,

I float slowly toward the rocking raft, haul
myself up, and lie on these

warm boards, exhausted as an enlisted
man after a day in boot
camp. This small pond in the woods of Maine is
my own training ground to test

how deeply I can plunge into this life,
how long I can last in that
other and survive to tell about them both.
I know the risks of going

and of coming back, but with my face turned
toward the blazing sun, I wait
until I'm prepared to climb this ladder,
to stand here on the tip of

this raft's high diving board, and, dizzy with
the mere possibility
of more being than any boy can know,
I leap again, and then again.

❈   ❈   ❈

Like cracks in the glaze
of heirloom cups that
pass through the hands of
generation after
generation of
mothers and daughters,
none ever knowing
why or when that glaze
crazed and each staring
more deeply at those
lines than her mother,

as if into her
own palm or mirror,
as if holding her
face in her own hands
tracing the hard and
deep passage of days
that left their mark on
the topography
of her brain, diverged,
and all but the scars
they left have been long
forgotten until
now, when her days start
to converge again,
like tears in her veined
eyes, to be restored
into some kind of
whole that she can hold
in her cupped hands so
the scattered meaning
of her light might be
finally released
from porcelain on this
blinding summer day,
while her man's at war,
while her daughters are
asleep and their dreams
of lonely daughters
etch themselves in the
ivory of their skulls,
the blue of their blind
irises, as images
are scored on the rim
of memory and yield
no more meaning
than utter presence,
like cracks in the glaze

of this heirloom cup
about to shatter
in your hands and eyes.

☒   ☒   ☒

Coppers, nickels, silver dollars tumble
from the incision in your
plastic piggy-bank. The alloy of their
light sprays around the living

room, scars our faces, hands and thighs, steams
windows with the breath of our
high, shrill cries over so much metal
money it could fill a hogshead.

Daphne, we worked hard to fatten
your pink pig, saved every scrap
of change we had for years, sometimes just to
rob it back for lunch money

or for dinner at McDonald's when
we were all too spent to cook,
until it became so heavy, it threatened
to buckle under its own

weight, topple, crash down through the kitchen floor
into the cellar, its coins
squealing the amazement of such fall, like
the cries of young soldiers.

Your mother leaves her studio, craft and art,
steel fabrications of her
tongue, brilliant metal objects she will sell
to galleries and museums;

radiant with satisfaction, she comes
to join us as we toast in
another year we have survived without
the world at war, without sons,

brothers, strangers shedding blood in nameless
fields, women teaching daughters
the hard songs of survival in the dark
around the kitchen stove, men

hard at work in a necessary kill.
For the life of all of us
our fathers slaughtered pigs, our mothers
made that dead meat and blood

into our common daily food. Tonight,
as candlelight shimmers in
the residue of wine and the echo
of pine needles starts to fade

in this new year's dark, Daphne, my dear
daughter, we do what mothers,
fathers must do in another time and place.
We sing you other songs.

Husbands and Lovers

In my father's house late every
afternoon, the men gathered in
the stable, where Uncle Larry

sold them amber jiggers of rye
whiskey, bootlegging them at fifty
cents a shot. And while Ely,

sullen, shoveled cow manure,
they yelled at him, the only perks
of that small barnyard sinecure.

As whiskey burned their throats, they sat
on milking stools, on sacks of grain,
just fucking this and fucking that

as men do when they are alone.
They told stories, each new shot of
rye cutting closer to the bone:

Cliff Wallace tricking Chet Lachance
into buying a dead horse; Grace
Gould naked at the grange hall dance.

One time George Farrar paid his own
uncle to seduce his wife so
he could divorce her, he had grown

so sick of her. Larry's bastards
littering the beds of strangers'
wives and sweethearts. . . so many shards

of misbegotten seed. "D'ya hear
how Duke, the barber, got beat up
by sailors, that cock-sucking queer,

his dyed hair and white Cadillac!
Well, they found 'im, black and blue and
bloody, almost dead, in the back-

seat of his car. I want to buy
my friend here one more drink before
. . . goddam, now I've forgotten why."

And if one pressed his luck a bit
to speak of what lay heavy on
his tongue, the others mumbled, "Shit!

Oh, shit!" — the white sound made by men
bred to be loveless all their lives,
lust flaring in them now and then

like coal-bin dust ignited by
the flint of foreign presences,
a lover's ghost, a shot of sky…

before they closed the stable door
behind them and drove off, not drunk,
just having died a little more.

❖   ❖   ❖

What did they know of love, these men
who spent their days in spinning rooms
or in cleaning out a pigpen

for the sow to have her piglets
in, then devour all of them
but two that Larry raised as pets

on gruel behind the kitchen stove
until he slaughtered them for food?
These men, what did they know of love —

my small father and his brothers
who, when not working, mined their own
silent hearts for warmth in winters

and on summer nights, as they sat
in their dark living room, alone,
or on the front porch where they spat

out the phlegm of their decaying
lungs, laced with their heart's bitter blood
in moonlight, while butts of burning

cigarettes died in the gravel
drives like life-supporting planets,
their wives, the echoes of their threats…
these men who knew so much of hell?

✠   ✠   ✠

We sit at the kitchen table
in the comfort of the semi-
darkness, smoking, barely able

to unearth love's tongue we've buried
for so long in these root-cellars
of our hearts. We won't be hurried

by pent-up pressures of lost years
that have imploded on themselves
(we start and finish two more beers)

like the flaring star-tips of our
cigarettes burning themselves out
far inside our lungs. This hour

calls for what our fathers never
learned: the courage to speak simply
of our love of one another

as two men who have survived the char
of our fathers' love, and as
the husbands, fathers that we are,

instead of burning up our lives
in cellars, factories or stables,
and damning our sons and wives.

Survival Skills

In order to become a wolf,
eventually a bear, and then,
one day, a full-fledged eagle
scout, you had to carve a duck
out of a bar of Ivory Soap —

carve with such craft that duck could float
upright in our den mother's dishpan
and swim, you'd swear, straight up
the bright October light streaming
down into her tiny kitchen

where we sat around the table,
a knife in one hand and a bar
of dry Ivory in the other. We
did that to rehearse survival
skills we'd need in the wilderness;

make decoys good enough to lure
whole flocks of ducks, and geese, and swans
in Fall, in high hunting season;
demonstrate we were ambitious
and mature enough to start this

project and to see it through.
My ducks would float but never swim.
I chipped and carved, carved and whittled:
they rolled over on their backs, and,
even if they had been genuine ducks,

would have drowned before dissolving
in a rush of sunlight and white froth.
Now Fall's upon us; leaves flutter;

hunters haunt the fields for quarry.
I have survived this long; I have

lured more than my share of barnyard
friendships and migrating strangers.
I've seen a few through to their deaths.
Still, here I am at that sullen
craft again. Sounds flash like marble

chips melting in sunlight, badges
glint, the eyes of mounted trophies;
and in this October's blinding
light that floods my room and foams,
I am that eagle. This is that duck.

A Momentary Order

He's spent this long hot morning
in my neighbor's yard. Where weeds
were so thick their thin stalks hauled
growing clumps of earth along
both sides of walks and their roots
stretched the limits of the earth
in affirmation of what
would outlast cement — the will
of chaos at the heart of
a more primal energy — he
carved clean, wide, precisely edged
and hosed-down paths gleaming toward
the center of a newer
and imagined world inside
the old. And he trimmed bushes:
spring's bright forsythias that
bloomed ecstasies of suns,
small galaxies of sharp and
yellow stars of burning sap
that swirled about themselves in
an orbit of fierce light and
threatened to become word, here,
in our backyard next to that
leaning fence — until the blooms
consumed themselves with the fire
of their breath, leaving small, black
open mouths in the tracery
of branches wild with photo-
synthesis; dark green cedars
that erected spheres of fragrance
shimmering above circles
of shorn limbs, pools of odor
all around themselves, around

him who released the geo-
metric symmetry of that
relentless upward thrust of
energy's green lava as
it vaults toward that dreamt-of cast
of form until the stunning
weight of its own shape plunges
it back down into itself,
only to leap up again
in ceaseless cycles of
impossibility, that
longer-lasting harmony
of atoms at the center
of each cedar standing in
a long straight line between my
neighbor's driveway and my own.

After he had taken off
his shirt, brushed his blond hair from
his brow, held the hose high in
the air, sprayed cold scrims of water
on himself, and as his
body shuddered aureoles
of steam, he began to prune
the fruit trees. He clipped each twig
draining power into space,
stripped off tough ophidian
vines that twisted into tight
and tighter coils, embedding
themselves in the bark until
in time the carcasses of
trees would be earth's monuments
to that bloody battle for
survival from the day a god
stood naked in the eye of dawn,
nameless in a nameless place,
and all creatures turned away

in shame, all but the two who
offered him their own nakedness,
the dim incarnate echo
of his voice reverberating
in them even after he
had recognized the pure light
of his beauty in the swirl
of atomic particles
in their muscle, bone and blood,
in the spinning nebulae
of eggs and sperm, the kelson
of his image, and he had
banished them to silence, cut
off from his breath by a sword
blazing like a cedar — and
was reverberating still
in this young man's body and
my own, as he stepped into
an oasis of green leaves,
absorbing this bright morning's light
to transform it into shade,
and gazed at the trees with such
satisfaction that small buds
of germinating fruit seemed
about to throb with a promise
in their pulp that had lain dormant
since that long-forgotten time
when clustered seeds inside their
core felt a naked presence
in the morning air, much like
the one that was stirring now,
there, among my neighbor's trees,
well beyond my reach and call.

As he ambled toward his morning's
final task, the garden at
the center of my neighbor's

yard, his features had become
resplendent with abandonment —
a spray of light grounded in
the pool of hair above his
groin, surging in a single
jet of brilliance, fanning out
across his chest and pulsing
its reflection on his face,
a borealis of oblivion —
as if he wasn't just
a hired hand, as if he
wasn't simply cleaning up
a backyard left untended
far too long, as if he too
believed the myths and meta-
phors I was projecting on
him and his work, transforming
it into that more substantial
truth of art when all is still
epiphany, not sluggish
fact transmuted into act.

And I wanted to intrude.
I wanted to run out, storm
my neighbor's fence and shatter
the illusion of that once
pure, contained and human place
being recreated here, today,
in suburbia outside
Rochester, New York, reason
with him to abandon this
pursuit of some perfected
vision to reverse, right now,
the thrust of entropy at
the heart of all we are and
do — just beg this boy to go
and leave well enough alone.

We have long been civilized
by creature comforts and the
absences of hope that we've
sublimated into small,
neurotic habits of a
slow, diurnal suicide,
and we're vaguely reconciled
with living with the silence
of our sterile cedars' waste
of energy on dark and
interlocking limbs that block
our neighbors from our sight, with
our driveways and our walks all
overgrown with healthy weeds,
like ancient aqueducts that
moss has muted or the paths
in forgotten cemeteries
where once-harnessed chaos
has returned to brute chaos
catapulting toward that promised
peace ruling at the heart of
stasis, and with our lovely wives
whose love has hardened into
bristling tolerance of our
touch as we brush against each
other — two famished panthers
prowling in the desert —
and who, in a crumbling beam
of light on waning after-
noons while ice cubes calmly crack
in the spectral well of their
martinis, are lovelier
as they become momentary
memories of their former selves,
their bitterness released like
lunar blood, their eyes uncoiled
and closed upon a dream whose

dream stirs in our sleeping genes
entangled in the roots of
a silence that still blooms in
our dark mouths, cross-pollinates
each time we speak, and, in rhythm
with our breath, scatters seeds that
flourish like our own sullen
children whom we raised in that
somber arboretum we
constructed (with the air and light
and moisture, the whole atmo-
sphere scientifically
controlled) to guarantee
endurance, when that world within
our world we had imagined
and designed and labored to
erect — during those brilliant
mornings when our whole bodies
ached with a hum that threatened
to explode into static —
collapsed: like echoes of a word
uttered centuries ago
and imploding on the fire
at its core; like this language
fired to inhuman pitch,
sentences pronounced in vain
against the tyranny of
gravity and space; like
planets burning themselves out;
or just like that young worker's
construct in my neighbor's yard
and in my line of vision
might have crumbled all around
him (as he knelt and stared
into the flower garden
as if seeing multiple
reflections of himself) had I

simply closed my eyes, focused
on some business near at hand,
and let him do the job that
he was being paid to do.

But, you see, already he's
begun to yank tall shafts of
wild grasses, panicles
of seeds hovering above
those corollas blooming in
the sprawling flowerbed; he
gathers faded ones and lays
them on his knees, gently,
as if once, even in this
life — last night, perhaps, as he
dreamed his own limbs were brilliant
petals of the cereus
unfolding into bloom,
a cup of moonlight glowing
in the desert night — he'd been
those flowers' unremembered
sister; off others he gleans
beetles as, in a desert
dawn and from the tips of thorns,
girls might pluck dewdrops cautiously
with their translucent finger-
nails. He leans closer to the dark
and moisture of the earth at
the center of the flowerbed —
where the languid laboring
of snails goes on just as surely
as the loud parabolas of
bees humming loads of pollen
overhead, just as surely as
the orbits of wild planets
and their moons in uncharted
space, or atoms in the tip

of each hair that illumines his
worn body — and he fills his lungs
with the cool green breath of moss.

He uproots a few last clumps
of weeds; his morning's work is
done; satisfied, he smiles, while
outside his eye's periphery
unfolds that drama he has
yet to learn: to strip oneself
of memory, desire,
all ambition to achieve
that bold serenity in
the homicidal coupling
of the praying mantis who
decapitates her mate, even
as he fertilizes her.

With his bare back and chest re-
fracting as much sun as they've
absorbed, he has labored with
the patience of a man obsessed
with the meticulous details
of a vision that would change
the world. As if denying
our history, our species'
and his own just by dint of
long, painstaking toil in bright
clouds of pollen he has raised,
its galaxy of micro-
scopic seeds clinging to his
body's salty, gentle sweat,
all morning he's imposed an-
other, momentary, but
perhaps more precious, order
on our all-too-resilient
and suburban wilderness.

He stretches in the total
shade of my catalpa tree,
he falls asleep and dreams, and
while the factory whistles blow,
while cicadas sing a high,
pure, unbroken ring of sound
around my neighbor's garden
and my own, suddenly the sun
this young man has absorbed all
morning long begins to rise,
to vault from his bare chest and,
in the center of his dream
in the center of my eye,
roots a blinding rib of light.

Irises

The beautiful wild irises we picked
along the back roads to our villa are
still alive in our landlord's earthen jug.
As purple as rinsed grapes, lemon yellow,
chestnut brown, their brilliance dominates

the foreground of our friend's photograph,
which is slightly out of focus, for his hands
were trembling that day, as if he were
witnessing the dawn *and* twilight of creation
in our modest back yard in Provence.

Just beyond the irises, an antique
wagon with a broken wheel, useless now
except as a planter for geraniums
rooted in the blood of sacrificial sons,
ravaged daughters, warring brothers;

nearby, a soldered swing-set rusting
in the acid laughter of lost children.
Then in the background, me: my chin resting
nonchalantly on my wrist, my straw hat
tipped at a rakish angle, and, behind

round red spectacles, the wild irises of my eyes
staring out directly at the trembling lens.
And oh, love, look: against a field of
brilliant poppies, the azure of the sea,
I am vanishing in ravenous light!

Flute Making

Cleave it, then,
trim off the leafy end,
those tough and bitter greens.
Wash it off and boil it
till the meat is bleached.

Take that clean bone
to the trembling desert
of the highest rooftop
and set it out to dry.

Keep watch over it.
Sit cross-legged and serene
in your most perfect lotus
moving with the sun and moon.
Let no shadow dampen it.
Beware of birds.

Let the sun dry out
the marrow. Lift the bone
up to your lips, gently
suck the powder,
and with your breath's
open hand scatter its dry seeds.

Let the bone dry still,
still more. Let it dry until
it glows, until your eyes
are burning jets of fever.

And when the sun
and moon are burning
in the same blue eye,

when seeds clatter
in your hip,
when your tongue
is bone, when the bone
is pure and dry,

then hone one end
until it's smooth
against your lips,
until your tongue
is comfortable on it.

Carve out the stops,
absolutely round.
Decorate it:
exquisite scrimshaw
from a perfect tusk.

Now play it.
Make music.
High, pure notes,
inhuman octaves.

Love, play
that fine flute
of my right arm.

Totem

Year in, year out, I've shed my skin
and hair, my teeth and sperm,
perfect invisible antlers. Animal,
I've molted friends and names.

Bones of strangers blow like bugles.
Hands ring. Tongues roll. A mob
of admiration starts to break and crush.

My ghosts roam the streets and wail.
I am arriving to myself.

Easter Sunday

All moisture's been sucked out of me.
I've turned in and on myself. Layers
of stale pastry, my skin flakes: Buddha
crumbling at last and falling into place.

In the basket of my dust, my friends
will find what was twisted in me,
always grating on my ribs: a thin
and indestructible scroll, undecipher-

able ancient characters I could never
understand: *You will live forever.*

ACKNOWLEDGMENTS

In Advent. E.P. Dutton & Co., Inc. 1972.
A Momentary Order. Graywolf Press. 1987.
Cave Dwellers. Graywolf Press. 1991.

Grateful acknowledgment is made to the editors of journals in which these poems, often in earlier versions and with different titles, first appeared:

The Atlantic Monthly; Boundary 2; Caim; Chelsea; Chicago Review; Choice; College English; December; Denver Quarterly; Esquire; The Iowa Review; The Kenyon Review; Mid-American Review; New American Review; New Directions; New England Review/Bread Loaf Quarterly; New Letters; The North American Review; The Ohio Review; Poetry Northwest; Poetry Now; Prairie Schooner; Rapport; Salmagundi; Shenandoah; Strivers' Row; Tar River Poetry; Thunder Mountain Review; West Hills Review; Williwaw.

The inscription for and all italicized lines and stanzas in the poem "Letters from the Tower" are from a poem by Robin Morgan entitled "White Sound" (*Depth Perception*, Doubleday & Company, copyright 1982 by Robin Morgan, and *Upstairs in the Garden: Poems Selected and New 1968–1988*, W.W. Norton & Company, Inc., copyright 1988 by Robin Morgan), reprinted here with the permission of the author.

ABOUT THE AUTHOR

A. Poulin, Jr. (1938-1996), was born of immigrant Québécois parents in Lisbon, Maine. He received a B.A. from St. Francis College, an M.A. from Loyola University, and an M.F.A. from the University of Iowa. He taught for the European Division of the University of Maryland, at the University of New Hampshire, and at St. Francis College, where he was chairperson of the Division of Humanities. In 1971 Poulin joined the faculty at the State University of New York, College at Brockport, where he was Professor of English. In 1980 he was Visiting Fulbright Lecturer in Contemporary American Poetry at the Universities of Athens and Thessaloniki in Greece.

A poet, translator, and editor, Poulin wrote a number of books of poetry, including *In Advent* (1972), *The Widow's Taboo: Poems after the Catawba* (1977), *A Momentary Order* (1987), and *Cave Dwellers* (1991). His books of translations include *Selected Poems* (1987) and *Day Has No Equal but Night* (1994) by the Québécois poet Anne Hébert, and *Duino Elegies and The Sonnets to Orpheus* (1977) and *The Complete French Poems* (1986) by Rainer Maria Rilke. Poulin edited the influential anthology, *Contemporary American Poetry* (1971), now in its Seventh Edition (with Michael Waters, 2001). He also edited *A Ballet for the Ear: Interviews, Essays, and Reviews* by John Logan (1983) and, with David A. DeTurk, co-edited *The American Folk Scene: Dimensions of the Folksong Revival* (1967).

For his poetry and translations, Poulin received both a creative writing fellowship and translator's grant from the National Endowment for the Arts, as well as a poetry fellowship from the New York Foundation for the Arts, two translation awards from Columbia University's Translation Center, and a Faculty Enrichment Programme grant for research and translation from the Embassy of Canada. In 1989 Poulin was awarded an honorary Doctorate of Humane Letters by the University of New England.

A. Poulin, Jr. was also the founding editor and publisher of BOA Editions, Ltd., an independent publishing house of American poetry and poetry in translation, celebrating its twenty-fifth anniversary in 2001.

BOA EDITIONS, LTD.:
American Poets Continuum Series

Colophon

The publication of this book was made possible, in part,
by the special support of the following individuals:

Philip Booth
Nancy & Alan Cameros
Carol Cooper & Howard Haims
Dr. William & Shirley Ann Crosby
Peter & Suzanne Durant
Richard Garth & Mimi Hwang
Bob & Rae Gilson
Dane & Judy Gordon
Don & Marge Grinols
Peter & Robin Hursh
Robert & Willy Hursh
Meg Kearney
X. J. Kennedy
Fred & Rose-Marie Klipstein
Archie & Pat Kutz
Rosemary & Lew Lloyd
Robert & Francie Marx
Kalliopy Paleos
Boo Poulin
Deborah Ronnen
Annette & Aaron Satloff
Jane Schuster
Pat & Michael Wilder
Helen & Glenn William

This book was set in Carter & Cone Galliard with
titles set in Mantinia. Both faces were designed
by Matthew Carter.

The interior was designed by
Valerie Brewster, Scribe Typography.

The cover was designed by Daphne Poulin-Stofer.

Cover art: *AP* by Robert Marx, courtesy of the artist.

Manufacturing was by McNaughton & Gunn,
Saline, Michigan.

BOA Logo: Mirko.